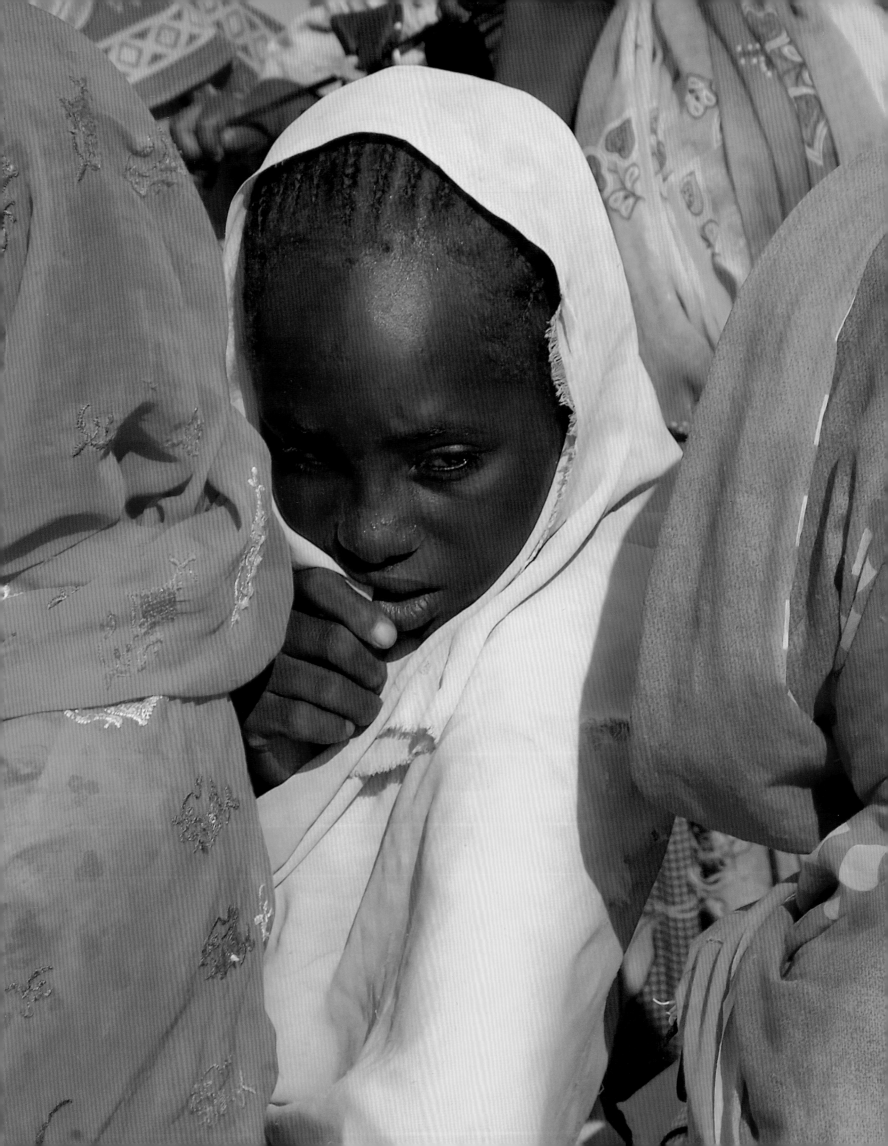

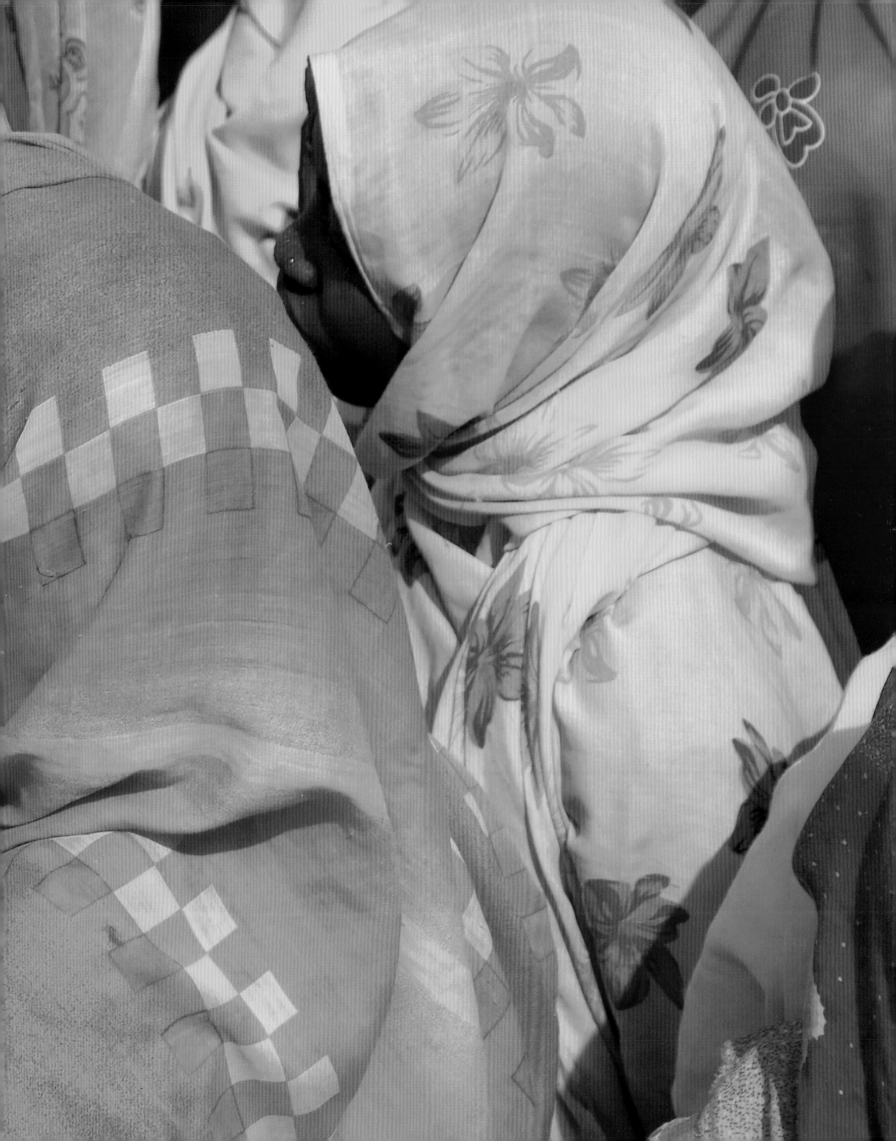

FOREWORD

Sudan is the most ethnically, geographically, and culturally diverse country in Africa. Yet most people only think of it in terms of large-scale suffering and seemingly endless strife. Hundreds of ethnic groups form a mosaic of Arab and African; Muslim, Christian and animist; nomad and farmer. The brutality of nearly fifty years of civil wars and a succession of humanitarian crises have retarded economic development and obscured the possibility of creating a truly plural society. The peace agreement of January 9, 2005, brings an unprecedented opportunity for the people of Sudan to put violence behind them. Despite the enormous challenges, there is now the chance for all Sudanese to forge new ways to share the natural, cultural, and historic bounty of their country, living together in peace and mutual respect.

The Carter Center is deeply committed to alleviating suffering in Sudan and helping to find ways to foster a lasting peace among its various peoples. In addition to supporting the peace process, the Center has been working to eradicate Guinea worm disease throughout the country and control river blindness along the tributaries of the Nile. I have witnessed the heartfelt desire of Sudanese—be they Arab or African, fishermen or farmers, bricklayers or camel herders—for justice, peace, and a better life for their children.

Michael Freeman's camera has caught the essential humanity in Sudan. He reminds us that life even in the most difficult times has its joy and that children must be nourished and pushed to achieve their very best. The striking parallels and borrowings of north from south and south from north should shake every Sudanese as well, adding to the recognition that, like all people, they are more similar than different and, in the end, all want much the same future for themselves and their families.

I am very pleased to see this book and am certain it will broaden understanding of Sudan, not only outside the country, but among Sudanese themselves. This understanding is vital if the country is to begin to realize its potential.

PREFACE

We are often asked why we decided to do this book. The short answer is that we believe only photographs can convey the geographic and ethnic diversity of Africa's largest country. Sudan's problems and its possibilities are far more complex and its people, like people everywhere, are far more complicated than press accounts can convey. Good pictures really are worth thousands of words, and we knew that our friend Michael Freeman was the photographer to take them.

When we landed in Khartoum on a hot August night in 1995, the official relationship between the United States and the government of Sudan was at a nadir. The Department of State had put Sudan on its list of state sponsors of terrorism because the country was hosting an alphabet soup of militant Islamic groups from throughout the Middle East and North Africa. Anti-American demonstrators periodically took to the streets. The American staff at the embassy had assumed a bunker mentality. As we moved into the U.S. ambassador's residence, we expected a very difficult time.

Within days, however, we discovered that Sudanese, whether rich or poor and from every region, are among the world's most gracious people. The warm welcome started with Sudanese employed at the embassy. These men and women, representing nearly every ethnic group in the country, are among the best educated, most thoughtful, and hardworking individuals anywhere. They provided our first glimpse into a multicultural society full of contradictions, where the poorest man will offer a stranger his last teaspoon of sugar and where more than a million people had died during decades of civil war.

Sudanese are renowned for their hospitality and extend it from the markets to the universities, from the churches and mosques to the homes of leading businessmen and politicians. Merchants in Sudan's *suqs* offer cardamom-laced coffee along with lively conversation about politics and religion. The late Shaykh Hasan Qariballah, leader of the Sammaniyya Sufis, invited us to attend a *dhikr,* the vigorous Friday recitation of the ninety-nine names of Allah, and allowed us to stand together in observation despite the fact that men and women usually worship separately.

When we first arrived in Sudan, the government militantly pursued a political Islamist agenda that included some heavy-handed proselytizing and limits on the building of churches. Yet, the Episcopal, Catholic, and Coptic cathedrals and churches around the country held services every Sunday. The government has always officially recognized Christian as well as Muslim holidays. Today, Muslim Sudanese express their welcome for Christmas holidays as Christians and Jews congratulate Muslims at Eid, the Islamic fast-breaking festival.

At every turn we found highly educated men and women due to the well-established schools and universities in Khartoum. The first secular school for girls, founded by Sudanese educator Babiker Badri, opened in 1907. It expanded over the decades to become the first indigenously founded women's university in Africa, and its forty-five hundred students include women from all over the country.

The Sudanese connection to the West is broader and deeper than we ever imagined. The Romans fought and traded with the kingdom of Kush. The Vatican sent Franciscans to the Funj capital, Sennar, in the seventeenth century, and the French doctor Jacques-Charles Poncet recorded a good description of that city in 1699. The Scot James Bruce traveled through the Funj kingdom on his trip to Ethiopia, leaving a good account of matters there in 1772. The distinguished French archaeologist Frédéric Caillaud accompanied Ottoman invading forces in 1820 as an observer. Among Americans, traveler and writer Bayard Taylor carried his country's flag to Khartoum in 1853, and President Theodore Roosevelt visited in 1910, stopping at the American Presbyterian mission on his way down the White Nile. In modern times, Sudanese study in Europe, the United Kingdom, the United States, and Asia. Trade and oil are enhancing ties with Asia.

Over the last decade we have met with everyone from the president, cabinet ministers, and opposition leaders in the north to southern intellectuals and rebel commanders. In some ways they are mirror images of each other. At their best, these men and women, polite and generous, intelligent and courageous, deeply religious, victims of brutalizing conflict, talk of their desire for a just peace and the struggle to make the political leap of faith to achieve it.

The pictures in the following pages seek to shed light on the rich ethnic tapestry of Sudan, to give historical context to its internal conflicts, and to show that Sudanese may have as much that unites as divides them. Peace is in process, and this book may contribute in some small way by increasing understanding both inside and outside of Sudan.

Timothy Carney and Victoria Butler

LIBYA

EGYPT

Red Sea

Dal
Dal Cataract
Sai Island
Soleb

Nile

3rd Cataract Tumbus
Kerma

Dongola

River

Karima 4th Cataract 5th Cataract
Old Dongola Jebel Barkal
El Kurru

Ariab

Port Sudan
Suakin
Erkowit

Atbara

Atbara River

CHAD

SUDAN

6th
Cataract

Meroe
Musawwarat-
es-Sufra
Naqa

Omdurman Khartoum
North

Khartoum ★

Jebel Aulia
Dam

White

Wad Medani

Kassala

ERITREA

Qadarif

Um Dalam

Geneina

Jebel
Marra
Mts El Fasher

Nyala

En Nahud

El Obeid

Babanusa

Kegel al-Khail
Keilak Kadugli

Nuba
Mts

Nile

River

Sennar
Sennar Dam

Dinder
National
Park

Kenana

Blue

Er Roseires
Damazine Roseires
Dam

Nile

River

Bahr al-'Arab River

Bahr al-Ghazal River

Heglig

Kodok

Malakal

Sobat River

ETHIOPIA

Bentiu

SUDD

Bahr al-Jabal River

Jonglei Canal

Pibor River

Akobo

Pochalla

River

CENTRAL
AFRICAN
REPUBLIC

Wau

Rumbek

Bor

Pibor
Post

Boma
National
Park

Iiti

Tambura

Terekeka

Boma
Plateau

Nzara Maridi
Yambio

Juba

Kapoeta

Lokichokio

Nimule

DEMOCRATIC REPUBLIC
OF THE CONGO

UGANDA

KENYA

*Undoubtedly unity is a laudable goal, but the best
guarantee for unity is for the leadership, especially
at the national level, to rise above factionalism and
to offer to the entire nation a vision that would inspire
a cross-sectional majority of the Sudanese people,
irrespective of race, ethnicity, region, or religion, to
identify with the nation and to stand together in
collective pursuit of their common destiny.*

—Francis Deng, Dinka scholar

CHAPTER ONE THE HISTORY

Sudan has never been an easy place to govern. Even those who have loved it the most have been frustrated by its complexity. Charles Gordon, Ottoman Egypt's governor-general, whose passion for Sudan cost him his life in 1885, lamented that "the Sudan is a useless possession, ever was and ever will be. . . . It cannot be governed except by a dictator who may be good or bad." Over the millennia Sudan's dictators came in the guise of pharaohs, monarchs, sultans, chiefs, foreign generals, and nationalist autocrats. None could exercise consistent central control over the entire country.

In the five decades since independence, every Sudanese government has struggled, mostly unsuccessfully, to articulate a national vision, rule a united country, and maintain good relations with neighbors. Differences in ethnicity, religion, and education have long threatened to splinter the country into fractious smaller states. Nevertheless, history has produced something uniquely Sudanese, a complicated blend of countless ingredients that have maintained their individuality even while taking on a communal flavor. With the formal end to the long civil war between the north and the south in early 2005, Sudanese leaders have the opportunity to develop a government that will, for the first time, be responsible to its entire people.

Ancient History

Thirty archaeological missions are currently excavating Sudanese sites that date from the early Paleolithic period to just a few hundred years ago. Each year their discoveries increase our understanding of Sudan's unique contribution to early civilization and put critical current problems, such as resource allocation and ethnic rivalry, into historical perspective. The excavations at Sai Island in the northern Nile, for example, may hold the key to understanding the transition from the last groups of *Homo erectus* to the emergence of *Homo sapiens*. The late French archaeologist Francis Geus and his team working at Sai have found several distinct

The interior of the *qubba* of
Shaykh Idris Mahgoub, at
Kueka on the northern Nile,
built to house the remains of
this nineteenth-century Sufi
holy man of the Khatmiyya sect.

layers of civilizations, one piled on top of another. One of their finds, a stone for grinding rock pigments, is more than a quarter-million years old and suggests the existence of a well-rooted and fairly advanced culture. Geus's team has also found the remains of Stone Age flake and core tools, Egyptian and Napatan kingdom graves, Christian cathedrals, and Ottoman Turk structures dating well into our era.

Humans were widespread across northern Sudan by the middle Paleolithic, seventy thousand years ago. Within another twenty thousand years, a time of enormous climatic flux, they had formed separate cultural groups in the Nile River Valley. Fossils and rock engravings of giraffe, elephant, and other wild game are evidence that a wide variety of flora and fauna once flourished in what is now one of the most arid places on the planet.

Near Kerma, Swiss archaeologists recently unearthed hunting and fishing cultures dating to the Mesolithic era, some ninety-five hundred years ago. Grave sites have yielded hourglass-shaped stone lip-plugs, which were inserted into the upper or lower lip for decoration, a custom still practiced in parts of southern Sudan. During this period, in the region between the Atbara River and Khartoum, an early Khartoum civilization began firing clay, creating a distinctive wavy-line pottery.

By the Neolithic period, between 4900 and 3000 BCE, groups in the Sahara, organized primarily as chiefdoms, were making sophisticated pottery that added bottles and plates to the earlier production of bowls. They also domesticated animals and raised subsistence crops. Cattle herding became, as it remains for much of Sudan today, a way of life. The earliest examples of bead jewelry and shells used for decoration come from Neolithic graves. As the region began drying up, people gradually shifted toward the Nile.

The Kingdom of Kush

Ancient Nubia covered most of northern Sudan and what is now southern Egypt. Here, around 3700 BCE, an indigenous culture centered between the First and Second Cataracts of the Nile produced a fine eggshell pottery and traded with Egyptians to the north. A few hundred years later, somewhat farther south, another more important Bronze Age civilization, the Kerma Culture, named for the modern village at the site, developed from preexisting late Neolithic groups. Known to the Egyptians as Kush, it is now believed to be the first great black African kingdom. Charles Bonnet, a Swiss archaeologist who has supervised

excavations at Kerma since 1973, says he came to the site to find Egypt but instead found Sudan's own history and early civilization.

A largely agricultural society, the people of Kerma had a very close relationship with their animals, as do many Sudanese peoples in our present era. Some cattle horns in one Kerma grave bear signs of man-made shaping, a practice that is ongoing among southerners. Townspeople organized themselves around centers of royal and religious power, the most prominent of which was the great mud-brick temple known as the Western Deffufa, to this day the largest ancient monument in sub-Saharan Africa.

At its height, from 2500 to 1500 BCE, Kush ruled an area stretching perhaps twelve hundred miles along the Nile, from the Fifth to the First Cataract, just north of Sudan's present border with Egypt. Kush developed an extensive commercial network, importing ivory, ebony, wild animals, and resin from the south to trade with Egypt. The Egyptian New Kingdom pharaohs conquered and held Kush for five hundred years, from 1500 to 1000 BCE. One key Egyptian temple, at Soleb on the west bank of the Nile, documents Amenhotep III's fourteenth-century-BCE victory over neighboring peoples. The bound captives shown on his temple's columns are clearly black Africans.

Around the eleventh century BCE, new indigenous forces began taking advantage of Egyptian weakness. Within 250 years they forced out the conquerors and took over Egypt itself. Thus, nearly three thousand years ago, Kush gave Egypt a pharaoh and its 25th Dynasty. The center of the renewed kingdom, Napata, remained the capital of a state that borrowed heavily from Egyptian culture. Its rule may have briefly stretched from the western borders of Palestine to the confluence of the Blue and White Niles. Napatan pharaohs chose to be buried at El Kurru and Nuri, both near their temple-mountain Jebel Barkal, next to the present town of Karima.

Egyptians eventually forced the Kush dynasty to retreat. Under increasing pressure, Kush leaders moved their capital south in about 300 BCE to Meroe. The Napatan necropolis, however, remained a burial site for Kushite rulers, including some well into the Meroitic period, suggesting a confused political and dynastic history.

The Egyptians themselves attached a special religious and cultural importance to Jebel Barkal, a plateau whose pinnacle on its southern aspect was thought to resemble a pharaonic crown with its uraeus, or cobra. The god Amun, they believed, resided inside the mountain, and

At Kerma, archaeologists found this cache of seven statues of pharaohs from Kush, of Egypt's 25th Dynasty.
Photo: C. Bonnet, Mission de l'Universite de Geneve au Soudan

they depicted him there in relief in a shrine dug into the mountain.

Among recent archaeological finds possibly related to resurgent Egyptian raids is a well-constructed pit found at Kerma and containing seven statues of Napatan rulers, including one of Taharqa, the leading Nubian pharaoh of the 25th Dynasty. All were broken as if to demonstrate the destruction of their powers but carefully interred, arguing that some regard for them still existed. Many years ago archaeologists found a similar desecration farther south at Napata itself.

Meroe

Although forced from Egypt, the kingdom of Kush continued to be a major power for more than a thousand years. Old, indigenous elements fused with Egyptian traditions to create, as they had done before and would do again, a new cultural synthesis on the Nile. Meroe, located between the Fifth and Sixth Cataracts, became the residence and the graveyard of the Kushite kings. The Meroitic kingdom represented the greatest state yet seen in sub-Saharan Africa, with perhaps the most extensive political structure in the area before the nineteenth century. This sophisticated civilization came into armed conflict with the Romans just before the time of Christ. Its craftsmen worked iron, outfitted baths with ceramic pipes, and covered the floors of palaces with elaborate tiles. The people of Meroe used a cursive script that replaced Egyptian hieroglyphics; it has been only partially deciphered, although the alphabet is known. The term "Ethiopian," first found in Greek and Roman accounts to refer to the people of Meroe, is derived from the Greek word for a sunburnt face. The Christian kingdom of Axum in today's Ethiopia finally destroyed Meroe about 350 CE.

The Christian Period

The empire of Kush gradually evolved into three Christian kingdoms: Nobadia, Makuria, and Alodia. Christianity probably took hold in Sudan through the conversion of ruling families. The people near the Nile practiced agriculture and those farther from the river lived as nomadic hunters and herders.

The first contact of these Nubian Christians with Islam occurred in the seventh century CE. The Christian kingdom of Makuria successfully resisted the Arabs who surged out of the Arabian Peninsula by negotiating a bilateral peace treaty known as the "Baqt." Under its terms, the Makurians agreed to provide tribute, including four hundred slaves a year, to the Arabs in exchange for goods such as grains, oil, and horses. The Arabs were free to travel but prohibited from settling in Nubia. Over time, however, many stayed. They intermarried, settled, and became part of an evolving culture. The two peoples, one primarily agrarian and living in established towns, and the other nomadic, coexisted fairly peacefully for more than five hundred years.

The rise of secular feudalism and internal strife led to the decline of the Christian kingdoms. Muslim scholars from North Africa and the Middle East arrived, establishing mosques and *khalwas,* schools to study the Qur'an. In 1323 a Muslim took the throne of the Makurian kingdom at Old Dongola.

French map from 1771 showing the kingdom of the Funj with its capital, Sennar. The toponym "Napata" persists in the kingdom of Dongola just south of "Turkish Nubia," at the easternmost bend of the Nile.
Authors' collection

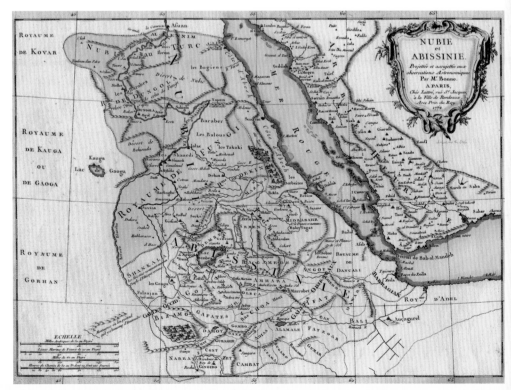

The Funj and Darfur Sultanates

The sixteenth century saw the rise of the first powerful Islamic state in the middle Nile Valley. The Funj, who probably originated in the east along the Blue Nile, ruled from Sennar in the region between the two Niles south of Khartoum. They joined with an Arab dynasty to destroy the last Christian kingdom and subsequently subjugated their Arab allies. The Funj controlled all the territory on the pilgrimage route from Kordofan in the west to Suakin on the Red Sea coast until 1821, when the sultanate fell to Turco-Egyptian invaders.

At the same time, another Islamic state had established itself in the far west in Darfur. International trade flourished along the Darb al Arba'in, or Forty-Days Road, that connects Darfur to southern Egypt. Darfur sent slaves to Egypt and had communications with both the Ottomans and Napoleon Bonaparte, who invaded Egypt in 1799. Pilgrims from as far away as Nigeria crossed through Darfur on their way to Mecca. Many stayed in Sudan, contributing to the ethnic mix.

The Turkiyya

The Ottomans took over Egypt in 1517. They did not, however, seek to control Sudan until centuries later, when Muhammad 'Ali Pasha became viceroy. He invaded Sudan in 1820 to remove the last vestiges of the Mamelukes, who had ruled Egypt during the previous centuries, and to tap Sudanese resources of gold and slaves. As he later wrote to his military commander, "You are aware that the end of all our effort and this expense is to procure Negroes." By the spring of 1821, the Ottoman army had seized control of the north, ushering in sixty years of colonial rule generally referred to in Sudan as the Turkiyya, or Turco-Egyptian period.

Muhammad 'Ali Pasha instituted a system of taxation on slaves and livestock so steep it amounted to confiscation. His intent was to commandeer strong male slaves to train as soldiers for his expanding army. The Sudanese balked, and one of the tribal leaders, Makk Nimr of Shendi, organized an uprising that killed the invasion commander, Muhammad 'Ali's son. This sparked a revolt up and down the Nile. Muhammad 'Ali, in a fury over his son's death, unleashed savage reprisals. Makk Nimr and his followers escaped into the mountains of Ethiopia, forming one of the first large refugee groups of modern times in the region. The Egyptians restored order only after some fifty thousand Sudanese had been killed.

Contemporary engraving of a portrait of the Ottoman governor of Egypt and conqueror of Sudan, Muhammad 'Ali Pasha.
Authors' collection

The new military governor of Sudan, 'Uthman Bey, immediately recognized the strategic importance of a strip of land at the confluence of the White and Blue Niles, where he built a fort and garrisoned troops. He called the place al-Khurtum, Arabic for "the elephant's trunk." The Dinka and Shilluk argue that the name comes from their word meaning "converging branches." Khartoum quickly became the colonial power's military and administrative capital. The Turkiyya built a civil administration, encouraged industrial and agricultural development, and expanded international trade. Suakin, on the Red Sea, served as the Ottoman gateway to Arabia.

The warlike Shilluk group and navigational hazards on the White Nile barred the way farther south for a while. In November 1839, however, a Turkish frigate captain led a well-armed naval expedition through the Shilluk area. Two years later, another expedition passed through the swamp known as the Sudd to reach the area of the Bari where Juba now stands. Exploitation of the south proceeded through trade in ivory and slaves.

The Slave Trade

Muhammad 'Ali took over Sudan largely to tap a reservoir of slaves for soldiers, concubines, and eunuchs. Once the Sudd had been penetrated, Egyptians established systematic and sustained trading networks with southern Sudan. Others quickly joined the predatory commerce. The early traders initially bartered for ivory, but they began to use force when they could not satisfy growing demand through peaceful exchange. Employing armed bands of northern Sudanese, the traders set up garrisons and pressed slaves into service as concubines, porters, servants, and, ultimately, private armies. The slave trade evolved as the garrison owners allied themselves with hostile ethnic groups that traded directly in slaves, sending caravans north along the White Nile as well as overland from the Bahr al-Ghazal region.

In the early 1850s, when the American traveler Bayard Taylor sailed 250 miles south along the Nile to a Shilluk village, he felt the enormous fear and ill will the slavers had engendered. Less than a decade later, when British explorer Samuel Baker set out down the Nile, relations between traders and indigenous ethnic groups had deteriorated into mutual distrust and violence. The lucrative slave trade eventually evoked a serious outcry from Europe, but not before it had ripped apart the social structure of southern and western peoples.

Antislavery idealism dovetailed with imperial ambition in the last decades of the nineteenth century. The Egyptian rulers appointed two Englishmen, first Samuel Baker in 1869 and later General Charles Gordon in 1874, to extend their administrative reach to Equatoria in the south and suppress the slave trade. Both failed. They had neither the military personnel to achieve their goals nor willing partners among southern chiefs, who in many cases had a financial stake in the trade.

The passionate and indefatigable Gordon, who became governor-general of all of the Sudan in 1877, was the first European and the first Christian to hold the post. In the same year the Egyptians, under pressure from London, concluded the Anglo-Egyptian Slave Trade Convention, which stipulated the end of the slave trade by 1880. Unfortunately for Gordon, he assumed power at a time when Khedive Isma'il, the Egyptian ruler he served, had neither the financial nor military resources to support him. The Khedive was ousted from power two years later, and Gordon resigned.

The Mahdist Revolution

The Muslim reformer Muhammad Ahmad ibn 'Abdallah sparked a revolution in 1881 when he sent letters to Sudanese notables announcing that he was the Expected Mahdi, the chosen leader dispatched by God to fill the earth with justice and equality. A student of several Islamic teachers and an initiate of the Sammaniyya Sufi order, he lived a militantly ascetic life on Aba Island in the White Nile, south of Khartoum. His followers believed him to be a holy man in possession of supernatural powers.

Muhammad Ahmad saw himself as a *mujaddid,* a renewer of religious faith, obligated to purge Islam of its faults. He claimed a unique status as the Imam, the Apostle of God. He tapped into the Islamic belief that in a time of crisis, a *mahdi* would appear to overthrow a corrupt order and set up a new theocracy. The Turco-Egyptian authorities, recognizing the danger posed by such a figure, sent a military expedition to Aba in August 1881 to capture Muhammad Ahmad, but the Mahdi's followers beat them off with spears and clubs. This victory over men with firearms enhanced the Mahdi's reputation for having mystical powers, and the number of his followers grew. He called them Ansar, after the original "helpers" of the Prophet Muhammad. The Ansar included religious men, ordinary citizens with real grievances among the central Arab groups, and Baqqara nomads anxious to cease paying taxes to a foreign power.

As chaos spread throughout Sudan, Charles Gordon was once again commissioned as governor-general. Shortly after arriving in Khartoum in February 1884, Gordon realized that it would not be possible either to make peace with the Mahdi or to successfully evacuate

Headquarters of the Mahdi at El Obeid, engraving.
From "The Land of the False Prophet," *The Century Magazine* (March 1885)

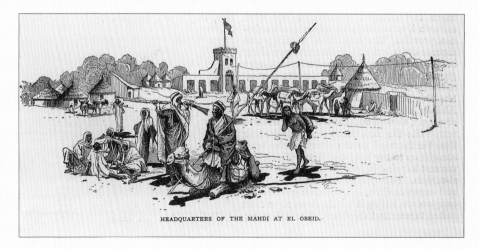

HEADQUARTERS OF THE MAHDI AT EL OBEID.

Egyptian troops. He called in vain on Britain to immediately send military reinforcements.

The Mahdi arrived across from Khartoum in October 1884 and made camp on the western bank of the White Nile in what is now Omdurman. A British relief operation arrived too late. The Mahdi's troops attacked Khartoum on January 26, 1885, and Gordon perished in the onslaught. The Mahdi made Omdurman his capital. Whatever his religious intentions, he had successfully united the northern tribes behind an Islamic ideology to drive out foreign rulers. In so doing, he laid the first foundation for the modern Sudanese state.

The Mahdi's larger ambitions to redeem the Muslim world went unfulfilled. He died just six months after the fall of Khartoum. His tomb, in the heart of Omdurman, remains an important landmark. Moreover, his descendants and those of his religious opponents, especially the leaders of the Khatmiyya Sufi sect, have played significant roles in the shaping of Sudan's politics over the last century.

The Khalifa

Following the Mahdi's death, a power struggle ensued within the Ansar. The tensions that surfaced between the religiously devout nomadic guerillas, the Sufi *tariqas* (sects), and the riverain elite who had formed the Mahdist army resurface regularly and resonate in conflicts still today.

'Abdallahi ibn Muhammad, a member of the Ta'aisha group from southern Darfur, emerged as the Khalifa, or successor, of the Mahdi. He shored up his political base by appointing kinsmen and clients to key command positions, and he resumed the holy war to extend the Mahdia in the west and on both the Ethiopian borders and the Egyptian frontier. That war has a modern echo, since it amounted to little more than a pacification of Darfur, where rebel Fur sought to reestablish their sultanate. One of Darfur's rebel leaders tried to legitimize his movement in Mahdist fashion by claiming that he was the third Khalifa. (Even today, rebel groups in Darfur employ Mahdist language, citing "justice and equality" to justify revolt.) As a matter of policy, the Khalifa, like the Mahdi, sought to keep the nomads close to his regime, turning them from casual raiders into a standing ethnic army. In the hundred years since, successive governments in Khartoum have followed a similar policy.

The Khalifa's troops scored some limited success on the Ethiopian border, but British-led soldiers soundly defeated them in the north. The south was increasingly restless. Moreover, an age-old enemy—drought—compounded the Khalifa's problems in the east and in Darfur. Like so many Sudanese leaders before and since, he had to deal with the simultaneous effects of poor policy exacerbated by a bad harvest, famine, and disease. After more than a decade, the British authorized Egyptian troops to march south toward Dongola as a counterpoint to French and Belgian activity in Central Africa. Anglo-Egyptian forces led by Herbert Kitchener reached Karari, just north of Omdurman, on September 1, 1898, and routed the Khalifa's forces, effectively ending Mahdist rule. Kitchener followed up this victory by facing down a French expedition at Fashoda (near modern Kodok) on the White Nile, thereby ending French imperial ambitions in the region.

Anglo-Egyptian Rule

The Anglo-Egyptian Agreement of 1899 called for conquerors Britain and Egypt to rule Sudan jointly through a Condominium administration based in Khartoum. At first, they relied on the old hierarchies established during the Turkiyya and Mahdist periods, thus reinforcing existing cultural, social, and economic divisions. In the north the Arabic language and Islam provided cohesion. Economic development focused on the Nile and its waters for irrigation schemes. Riparian communities benefited, but the policy tended to marginalize groups in border areas.

The sultanate of Darfur under 'Ali Dinar initially enjoyed autonomy. Caught between French colonial expansion on his west flank (in what is now Chad) and the

President and Mrs. Theodore Roosevelt at the Omdurman market, March 1910.
University of Durham, Sudan Archive

British to the east, 'Ali Dinar became increasingly agitated by the European colonial presence. When the Ottoman Empire entered World War I and the British responded by taking over Egypt, 'Ali Dinar called for a *jihad,* or holy war, against the infidel Europeans. The British moved against him and occupied his capital in May 1916. In an act that anticipated contemporary events, the British armed neighboring northern Arabs for reconnaissance into Darfur. Reginald Davies, director of British intelligence services, later wrote that these forces "were uncontrolled; and their vigorous interpretation of the term reconnaissance took them on forays not only into Darfur but across it, over a distance of perhaps three hundred miles or more . . . against their old enemies . . . from whom they looted not only animals but sundry human beings as well." Although 'Ali Dinar escaped, he was found six months later and killed.

Running counter to the centralizing trend of both the Turkiyya and Mahdist periods, the British implemented a system of indirect rule that initially depended on strong ethnic cohesion and leadership. At the same time they sought to reduce Egyptian influence in Sudan to prevent nascent nationalist demands for independence from spreading among educated Sudanese. Because they feared the nationalist aspirations of educated Sudanese, and because it was cheaper, the British chose to devolve administrative and judicial functions to ethnic authorities rather than form a modern governmental bureaucracy. Indirect rule also sought to minimize the political influence of religious leaders.

The policy had a profound impact in both the north and the south of Sudan. In the belief that modern education had created a discontented, "de-tribalized" modern class, the authorities began substituting *khalwas,* or religious schools, for government-supported elementary schools. Despite establishing additional facilities in Khartoum, including Gordon Memorial College, now the University of Khartoum, government support for education declined. In addition, the British opted to rule the "African" areas of southern Sudan separately from the north. In 1922 they established closed areas in an attempt to ensure suppression of any slave trade and to limit the spread of Islam. This effectively barred northerners from entering the south. The official policy was to leave local administration in the hands of native authorities. Where traditional organizations no longer existed, the British established chief's courts to mete out justice.

Postal First Day Cover commemorating the December 1948 opening of the first legislative assembly. Authors' collection

Southern Policy

Southern education under colonialism had been given largely to various Christian missionary groups, to which the south was parceled out much as the Pope had distributed New World territories to different Roman Catholic orders. Rather than creating a department of education, under its new policy the British increased grants to missionary schools and set out a few guidelines. They selected six languages to be used for instruction, promoted English as the lingua franca, and discouraged Arabic.

The southern policy thus encouraged the progressive separation of the south and fostered divisions within it. It was designed, as in the north, to thwart trends toward homogeneity. By 1930 the north and the south were almost completely isolated from each other, and communities within these regions had been segregated.

In 1934 Sir Steward Symes arrived in Khartoum as British governor-general. He adopted a new attitude toward the educated elite and began building an administration that would work in collaboration with Sudanese intelligentsia instead of ethnic authorities. Symes set about reforming education by establishing advanced schools for teacher training, law, engineering, medicine, veterinary science, and agriculture to meet the needs of government departments for technical talent.

Toward Independence

The Second World War had a much greater impact on Sudan than did the first. Italy, an enemy power, bombed Khartoum and briefly occupied Kassala near the border with Eritrea. The danger from the north continued until 1942, when British troops finally ended German aspirations to control the Nile Valley.

At this time, Sudanese political activists, who had banded together in the Graduates' General Congress, began pressing their demands for the right of self-determination. Under Isma'il al-Azhari and his political group, the Ashigga (literally "brothers by the same father and mother"), the Congress metamorphosed in 1943 into Sudan's first genuine political party and pressed for union with an independent Egypt. The Ashigga gained the support of Sayyid 'Ali al-Mirghani, the head of the Khatmiyya Sufi order whose dynastic history was closely connected to Egypt through its Turkiyya rulers. Meanwhile, another political wing, the Umma, was calling for complete independence for Sudan. Founded by supporters of Sayyid 'Abd al-Rahman, the son of the Mahdi, the Umma gained only limited popular appeal because of the party's apparent willingness to cooperate with the British and widespread concerns about the political ambitions of 'Abd al-Rahman.

In 1947 Britain accelerated its plans for wider Sudanese participation in the administration of the country and sponsored a conference including Sudanese from political and civic organizations. Its findings called for a legislative assembly and for replacing the governor-general's council with an executive council, half of whose members would be Sudanese. The recommendations forced the British to reconsider their policies toward the south, which, while designed to "protect" it, had also isolated it politically, economically, and socially. Pacification had taken longer in the south, and most of its people were economically poorer and far less educated than northern Sudanese.

In the same year, a conference in Juba produced the defining Condominium policy change. Sir James Robertson, the civil secretary, announced in 1947 that the south was "inextricably bound for future development to the Middle East and Arabia and Northern Sudan." He added that southerners should "be equipped to take their places in the future as socially and economically the equals of their partners of the Northern Sudan and the Sudan of the future." Southerners formed the Southern Liberal Party in 1951 and took part in 1953 elections in the south. But festering discontent resulted in a 1955 strike at the Zande

Flag-raising on Independence Day, January 1, 1956.
University of Durham Sudan Archive

cotton raising and textile scheme, and relations with the British remained uneasy. Nineteen fifty-five also saw a mutiny at Torit garrison which triggered the first phase of the civil war.

Meanwhile, Egyptian nationalists, also seeking independence from Britain, insisted that Sudan should be unified with their country. The 1952 Egyptian revolution paved the way for direct talks between Egyptian and Sudanese political parties. They agreed that self-determination should come first, with the election of a body to draft a new constitution to answer whether Sudan would be part of Egypt.

Sudan entered into a three-year transitional period of self-government in 1953. The National Unionist Party (NUP) won both chambers of the transitional parliament. The lower house voted unanimously to declare independence, a resolution the senate immediately adopted. The parliament then enacted a transitional constitution that gave the powers of the governor-general to a five-man supreme commission. The idea of union with Egypt died, a casualty of Gamal Abdel Nasser's rise and the reality that most Sudanese were opposed to being joined to their northern neighbor. On January 1, 1956, the flags of Egypt and Britain were lowered in Khartoum, and a new republic proclaimed. Recognized internationally, Sudan quickly became a member of both the Arab League and the United Nations.

Independence

An unstable coalition of rival political groups, the new government faced the immediate challenge of creating a constitution that acknowledged the religious and ethnic diversity of the country while expressing the will and aspirations of all Sudanese. At the same time, the government needed to maintain and expand the country's physical infrastructure, notably roads and railways; improve education; connect regions; and promote economic development. The main parties, however, could not agree on key elements of the national agenda and failed to allay the deep suspicions of southerners because all, except the Communists, wanted an Islamic constitution.

The 1958 elections went to Umma, but factionalism, allegations of corruption, and economic mismanagement fueled popular discontent. Toward the end of the year, the commander-in-chief of the Sudanese army, Major General Ibrahim Abboud, ousted the civilian government. In a pattern doomed to be repeated over three decades, he dissolved political parties, abolished trade unions, placed ministers under arrest, suspended the transitional constitution, and proclaimed a "democratic republic" with popular sovereignty, but without elections.

Abboud's singular success was in improving Sudan's relationship with Egypt. He signed a Nile Waters Agreement that included compensation to Sudan as well as approval for construction of the Roseires Dam on the Blue Nile. Egypt, always preoccupied with any development on the Nile, its sole source of water, saw the dam as compensation to Sudan for the lands lost to the reservoir that the Aswan Dam created. Nubians, however, unhappy with the Aswan flooding of their lands, sparked an opposition that only increased as the government failed to create sustainable economic and social policies.

Abboud's handling of the south set a range of grievances and distrust that is a reality of Sudanese politics to this day. Abboud continued to appoint mostly northern officials to southern posts and accelerated efforts to advance Islam and the Arabic language in the south.

Christians could not open new schools nor engage in missionary activity. In 1964 his government expelled foreign missionaries from the south.

Meanwhile, new political players, including the communists and the Muslim Brotherhood, had been coming onto the scene since the late 1950s. Many young educated Sudanese turned to these groups. Banned by the Condominium and by parliamentary and military authorities, the Communist Party operated through various fronts. The clandestine Muslim Brotherhood, founded in Egypt in the 1920s, had also been suppressed.

Important southern intellectuals and politicians left the country and formed an opposition movement—the Sudan African National Union (SANU)—based in Uganda. SANU became the voice of the thousands of refugees who fled the increasing instability of the south, where the government was warring with a rebel group known as Anya Nya. By 1963 some sixty thousand refugees had fled to Kenya. SANU asked for and received relief moneys from the United Nations, initially through its refugee relief agency, beginning a role that continued over the decades of civil war in the south.

The military government responded to these unsettled circumstances by appointing a commission to examine southern unrest and invited public discussion. This only served to rally a disparate coalition of students, teachers, and professional groups who opposed the regime. In the so-called October Revolution of 1964, Abboud was ousted.

Rebellion in the south and bitter feuding among political factions dominated the second parliamentary government. The 1964–69 period saw increased fighting in the south with atrocities committed by both government troops and the Anya Nya. At the same time a pattern of north-south negotiations with foreign observers began, the first a promising Round Table Conference in Khartoum in 1965. Northerners and southerners articulated the positions that would divide them for the next forty years. The north cited "evil colonial policies" and "hypocritical European missionaries." They proposed a regional administration for the south that would control education, public health, commerce, and agriculture, with the national government sovereign. SANU countered that southerners should decide through a plebiscite whether to have a union, federation, or independence. They also wanted control of finance, foreign affairs, and the armed forces in the south. The Round Table Conference agreed on some general principles to guide policy and established a twelve-man committee whose report later provided the basis for the ten-year suspension of the civil war negotiated at Addis Ababa. It did not immediately resolve the vital question of the south's constitutional status.

The unsettled situation effectively denied genuine southern representation in the 1966 elections. The two major parties—Umma and the NUP—once again formed a coalition. The minority Communists elected Sudan's first woman member of parliament, Fatima Ahmed Ibrahim, president of the Sudanese Women's Union. She was the first woman elected to parliament in any Arab or African country. The Sudanese Women's Union won the United Nations Human Rights Prize in 1993 for securing legislation that guaranteed women rights in the home, workplace, and politics.

The great-grandson of the Mahdi, Al Sadiq al-Mahdi, won his first election and, at age thirty-one, became prime minister. He lasted only nine months before parliamentary maneuvering brought down his government. Although Sadiq al-Mahdi initially wooed southerners, he ultimately alienated them by expressing support for an Islamic constitution in order to shore up his position within Umma. New general elections in 1968 produced a parliament with no political party in the majority. The new coalition, like the one before, failed to deal effectively with the economy or the war in the south and thus paved the way for another military coup.

The Nimeiri Period, 1969–85

On May 25, 1969, Colonel Jaafar Nimeiri and his Free Officers movement seized power swiftly and bloodlessly. Making arrests and restricting institutions and freedoms, Nimeiri promoted himself to major-general and justified the coup by castigating politicians who had failed to deal with the country's economic and regional problems. He set up a Revolutionary Command Council (RCC) and announced a "democratic republic" to advance independent "Sudanese socialism."

The Ansar, who had mended their internal differences, resisted. Imam al-Hadi, a grandson of the Mahdi, withdrew with his supporters to Aba Island, the spot from whence the Mahdi had launched his revolution nearly a hundred years before. In 1970 government troops launched an air and ground assault, killing thousands of Ansar. Al-Hadi was killed, and Sadiq, who had become head of the Ansar as well as the Umma Party, fled into exile.

Nimeiri stayed in power over the next sixteen years, ruthlessly playing one political group against another.

First to go were his early allies, the Communists. In 1971, responding to conservative pressure, he dismissed three from the RCC, purged others, and used anti-communist public rhetoric. Young, Communist-inspired military officers staged a coup in July 1971 and briefly jailed Nimeiri, but they lacked broad Sudanese support. Libya, Egypt, and the United Kingdom quickly intervened to support Nimeiri, who proceeded to purge his government and military of all leftists.

The southern rebellion grew as Nimeiri's early positive direction changed to an impulse to suppress the uprising militarily. Weapons, money, and sanctuary came from Ethiopia, Uganda, and Israel. As many as a half-million people may have died in the south in the 1960s. Northern politicians had long paid lip service to the idea of southern autonomy but still pressed for a unified Sudan that would form part of the Muslim Middle East.

Nimeiri finally recognized that waging war in the south was draining human and financial resources. In mid-1971 he appointed the southern magistrate Abel Alier, a Dinka, as minister of southern affairs and proposed peace talks. Alier succeeded a prominent southerner executed for his role in the attempted coup. At the time, southern soldiers and politicians themselves had come together in the Southern Sudan Liberation Movement (SSLM) under Joseph Lagu, who wanted to open talks with the government. A series of secret meetings culminated in a conference in Ethiopia in 1972 and the Addis Ababa Accords, which ended the war that year.

Under the peace agreement, southerners gained regional autonomy with charge of everything except national defense, foreign affairs, finance, interregional communications, and the national tasks of economic and social planning. Southern rebels would be incorporated into the army. Arabic was the official language, but English would be the main language in the south. Nimeiri appointed Abel Alier as first president of the High Executive Council for the south. He eventually became vice-president of Sudan and recently advised both the government and rebel delegations that negotiated the peace agreement signed in Kenya on January 9, 2005.

Nimeiri failed to gain broad northern support for the accords. Conservatives argued he had surrendered to southerners. As the years wore on, he spent his time maneuvering to stay in power rather than trying to build a national consensus. His economic policies exacerbated his problems. Inflation, mismanagement, and corruption resulted in an end to World Bank disbursements in 1981. The International Monetary Fund refused to provide emergency loans without strict austerity measures. Meanwhile hundreds of thousands of refugees arrived in Sudan from Ethiopia and what later became Eritrea, fleeing drought and famine, adding to the economic burden.

Nimeiri diluted the potential power of a unified southern bloc by dividing the south into three regions. This pitted southern leaders against each other. When the Regional Assembly finally rejected the proposal in 1981, Nimeiri dissolved the assembly, jailed opponents of his scheme, and unilaterally decreed the new structure. These moves further alienated southerners, already disillusioned because the economic and social benefits they had expected from peace had not materialized.

Nimeiri ensured a return to armed struggle by two additional actions: appointing the leader of political Islamists, Hasan al-Turabi, as attorney general and, in September 1983, imposing Shari'a, or traditional Islamic law, on the entire Sudan. A separatist group called Anya Nya II proclaimed itself. But the more serious defection was that of Colonel John Garang de Mabior, whose army battalion had revolted in the summer of 1983 and formed the Sudan People's Liberation Army (SPLA). They had assistance from Ethiopia's Derg regime and took over most of the south in the next three years.

Nimeiri's regime finally imploded from the combined effect of economic failure, civil war, famine, and widespread public disenchantment. A massive antigovernment strike secured Nimeiri's downfall while he was out of the country. In his absence, the army commander, General 'Abd al-Rahman Muhammad Siwar al-Dahab, announced the military would "yield to the wishes of the people." Nimeiri went into exile in Egypt. Dahab dissolved parliament, suspended Nimeiri's May 1973 constitution, and promised to end the civil war. He declared a cease-fire and offered an amnesty. Civil society met with the SPLA abroad, producing the Koka Dam Declaration that called for a Sudan "free from racism, tribalism sectarianism, and all causes of discrimination and disparity." But Dahab could not mobilize the north to repeal Shari'a laws. He did, however, follow through on a promise to return power to civilians in a year.

The government that resulted from the April 1986 elections lasted only three years. Umma won the most seats and its leader, Sadiq al-Mahdi, formed another coalition that included his Khatmiyya rivals in the Democratic Unionist Party (DUP). As they fell out, Sadiq moved closer to the official opposition, the National Islamic Front (NIF), the latest evolution in the political Islamist movement.

The leader of the DUP, Muhammad Osman Mirghani, met in Ethiopia with SPLA leader John Garang in 1988. Their ceasefire agreement centered on the suspension of the Shari'a laws, a move Mirghani tried to convince others in Khartoum to take. Prime Minister Al Sadiq al-Mahdi dissolved his government and formed a new coalition committed to implementing the 1988 DUP-SPLA agreement.

In March 1989, after initial resistance, the Sadiq al-Mahdi government reached agreement with the United Nations and donor nations on a plan called Operation Lifeline Sudan under which desperately needed food moved into SPLA-controlled and government areas of Sudan. The plan limited deaths from starvation and became the basis for a combined food and medical effort vital to relief throughout the south. As Sadiq al-Mahdi, under military urging, moved forward with plans to hold a consultative conference with southerners, forces opposed to any reduction in the role of Islam intervened.

Political Islam

On June 30, 1989, acting under the instructions of the Islamist Movement, Brigadier 'Umar Hasan Ahmed al-Bashir overthrew the government in a bloodless coup and established a fifteen-member Revolutionary Command Council for National Salvation. The politically Islamist members of this latest RCC made allegiance to Hasan al-Turabi, leader of the Islamist Shura, then made up solely of members of the Muslim Brotherhood. The Islamist group initially prosecuted the civil war and associated itself with Islamist movements, including radical groups outside Sudan. Turabi believed Sudan could both spread political Islam internationally and support armed Islamist insurrection regionally. He invited Osama bin Laden and his "Afghan Arab" followers to live in Sudan.

In the mistaken belief that the government could achieve a military victory over the south, Turabi described the fight as a *jihad,* with casualties declared martyrs. The civilian death toll in the south mounted, as did the loss of northern troops, whose deaths contributed to northern opposition to the war. Tragically, young soldiers filled the graveyards of both north and south, leaving no family in either region untouched by personal loss and grief.

By early 1996 Sudan's neighbors were deeply suspicious of the authorities in Khartoum. The United Nations invoked sanctions against Sudan's diplomats and airline after an Egyptian terrorist group, operating from Sudan, attempted to kill the Egyptian president in 1995 as he landed in Addis Ababa. The United States had declared Sudan a state sponsor of terrorism in 1993 and imposed its own bilateral sanctions in 1997. Some among the ruling Islamists began to question both their international and domestic policies as well as the role played by Turabi. Osama bin Laden was expelled in May 1996. By December 1999 a split in the movement resulted in the eclipse of Turabi and a new direction in internal and external policies.

Meanwhile, internal conflicts were tearing at the SPLA and the political movement John Garang had created, the Sudan People's Liberation Movement (SPLM), as factions broke away and formed competing rebel movements. The Nasir Declaration of 1991 pitted Riek Machar and his Nuer followers with other leaders against the SPLA. The ensuing battles killed and displaced thousands. Many fled north to seek safety and jobs, flocking to camps surrounding Khartoum.

A series of international conferences sought to negotiate an end to the conflict. Under the aegis of the regional Intergovernmental Authority on Development (IGAD) and an associated body of foreign governments, the IGAD Partners Forum, Khartoum, fully accepted a "Declaration of Principles" in 1997, after three years of negotiation. The agreement gave priority to the unity of Sudan; secular, democratic, social, and economic systems; and equitable sharing of national resources. The issue of self-determination for the south remained outstanding. The peace process languished as IGAD members Eritrea and Ethiopia went to war in 1998.

In 2001 the situation was ripe for a new intervention. President 'Umar al-Bashir was newly reelected, and Sudan had responded to the concerns of a U.S. counterterrorism team that had visited the country during the last months of the Clinton administration. In early September 2001, President Bush appointed former Senator John Danforth as his special envoy to assist the peace process. The government of Sudan and the SPLM agreed to a cease-fire in the Nuba Mountains in June 2002 and a month later signed the Machakos Protocol, which set forth the principles for a peace agreement.

Negotiations began in August 2002 and, under Kenyan mediation, ended on December 31, 2004, with the signing of the last two protocols. Negotiators Dr. John Garang and First Vice-President 'Ali Osman Muhammad Taha signed the Comprehensive Peace Agreement on January 9, 2005. A coalition government is to implement the accord, which

calls for a six-year transition period, at the end of which southerners will have the right to vote on remaining in a united Sudan or opting for independence. John Garang will become First Vice-President in the new government.

First Vice-President 'Ali Osman Taha and SPLA/M Chairman John Garang share a joke at the signing of the Comprehensive Peace Agreement ending the civil war, Nairobi, January 9, 2005. Photo: Reuters/Antony Njuguna

Future

Sudan's new government faces formidable problems, not the least of which is the major political and humanitarian crisis that erupted in Darfur in February 2003. Two groups—the Sudan Liberation Army and the Justice and Equality Movement (JEM)—spearheaded the western rebellion using foreign money and arms. Scores of thousands have been left dead and more than 1.5 million people displaced, following brutal suppression. Human rights violations occurred on both sides but the government's use of nomad militias received broad condemnation. The new coalition government must address legitimate economic and political grievances of people ignored and badly treated by central authorities. At the same time, the national government must deal with rebel groups such as the JEM, which draws its very name from the words of the Mahdi himself and whose ideology seeks the violent overthrow of the government.

Perhaps the most important change in Sudan in the century since Charles Gordon lamented that the country was ungovernable is the nascent shift in thinking about southerners by those in the north. More and more are now beginning to recognize the extent to which southern blood runs through their veins and influences their culture. Some northern Sudanese today will claim a Dinka, Shilluk, or Nuer ancestor, or explain the African roots of northern music and dance. In discussion, the reality of Sudan's diversity is broadly recognized, as is the potential that synthesis could have for the future. Moreover, war has brought a huge influx of southerners into the northern workforce. Every business or industry of any size depends on an integrated workforce. Hilton Hotel employees in Khartoum jokingly refer to themselves as a miniature United Nations, with staff from every major ethnic group and region. The Hilton is no longer an exception, as most employers seek to diversify their staffs.

Technology and education are playing their parts. Communications are faster and easier. Long-distance learning and laptop commerce are creating opportunities. Mobitel, Sudan's mobile phone provider, gained a million subscribers in its first three years of operation. The network now covers every major town under government control, making for the first reliable communication between regions.

Increased educational opportunities, particularly private schools, have enhanced economic integration. Ahfad University, the oldest indigenously founded women's university in Africa, sets aside scholarships for southern women every year. Besides a general liberal arts education, Ahfad offers degrees in medicine, law, and business. Ahfad has been at the forefront of programs to promote understanding between women from all regions of Sudan, and it is not alone. Many other universities seek to provide equal educational opportunities for all Sudanese.

Parents in both the north and south see education as the stepping stone to success. Southerners understand the urgent need to redress the imbalance in literacy greatly exacerbated by the civil war. Teachers in the south make do however they can, turning churches and even the shade of mango trees into classrooms. In survey after survey, southern parents tell UNICEF that education for their children is the highest priority.

Arabic and English are in a complementary role in modern Sudan. While English is still favored, and some in the south have resented the enforced teaching of Arabic, the vast majority of an estimated four million southerners who live in the north speak at least some Arabic because it is a passport into the workforce. In villages across the south itself, primary-school teachers drill students in the Arabic alphabet for much the same reason. People from different ethnic groups often use Arabic as their common language. Roman Catholic priests, trained at the Comboni seminary in Khartoum, conduct church services in Arabic and English.

A young priest in Kodok village on the White Nile, whose services in Arabic are the most crowded, smiles at the irony that the language of the Qur'an has become the language of Christians too.

Sudan has always had a progressive and important group of northern and southern intellectuals ideologically committed to human and political rights for all Sudanese. Their numbers have grown substantially over recent years. In addition, northern politicians who went into exile either voluntarily or by force have over the past decade increasingly rubbed shoulders with southern political leaders. This was notably the case in the creation of the National Democratic Alliance (NDA), a northern insurgent opposition against Khartoum that joined all opposition parties together with the SPLA. NDA and Khartoum authorities signed a peace agreement in June 2005.

The 2002 Nuba Mountains cease-fire and the reduction of hostilities during negotiations enabled people to begin to patch the social and economic fabric of their lives. People returned to home villages in the Nuba Mountains and resumed planting sorghum. Southerners, long separated by battle lines, started moving more freely between government and SPLM villages. This unfolding process has facilitated trade and promises to improve health care throughout the south.

The Atlanta-based Carter Center has been working in Sudan since 1986. Part of its mission has been the control of debilitating diseases such as river blindness, the world's second leading infectious cause of blindness. In 1995 the center started the Guinea Worm Project with the aim of eradicating the waterborne parasite, prevalent in southern Sudan, which invades the body and painfully emerges through the skin. Since the cease-fire, rural health workers have been able to reach even the most remote areas. Remarkably, the incidence of Guinea worm in the south has declined by 92 percent since 1996.

The international community has a broad, sustained role to play in helping Sudan build its infrastructure and develop its human resources if the country is to enjoy a peaceful and prosperous future. The success of the peace process, however, will depend foremost on the political will of the majority of Sudanese. The international community can offer imagination, money, mediation, and monitoring of the process, but Sudanese must show the political will to recognize and embrace their country's ethnic, religious, and cultural plurality and diversity. Good leadership can make that happen. Sudan's success could be a model for Africa and the larger world.

Overleaf:
Sai Island in the northern Nile. Excavations here have unearthed evidence of cultures that go back more than 250,000 years, to the transition from *Homo erectus* to *Homo sapiens*.

A Swiss team is among more
than thirty archaeological
expeditions at work in Sudan.
At Kerma, on the northern Nile,
they are excavating remains
that date from the second half
of the third millennium BCE.

Sudanese workers at the
Kerma dig. Potsherds found
here date from the earliest
days through the Egyptian
New Kingdom invasion
of about 1500 BCE to the
Kushite restoration.

At Soleb, north of Kerma,
the temple of Amenhotep III
celebrated the Egyptian
18th-Dynasty conquest of
the region.

The remains at Kerma, above,
of the huge mud-brick *deffufa*
(an ancient Nubian term for
any imposing building). Nearly
22 yards high, this was the
great temple of the town.

Murals at El Kurru, the royal necropolis of Napata, the northern capital of the kingdom of Kush. Above, the heart of a pharaoh of Egypt's 25th Dynasty is weighed as the vulture goddess Mut looks on, and below, the hawk-headed god Horus leads the deceased pharaoh into the underworld.

At Tumbus, north of Kerma, a broken statue from the Kushite period lies by the main road that follows the east bank of the Nile.

Sunrise through a dusty haze over the temple of Amenhotep III at Soleb (1370 BCE). The features of a bound captive on one of the pillars, above, mark him as a black African.

The temple of Amun, opposite, at the foot of the Jebel Barkal plateau. Egyptians and Nubians believed the shape of the plateau, resembling the pharaonic crown, indicated that the god Amun dwelled within the mountain, making it among the holiest sites in Egypt and Kush.

Above, looking across the top of Jebel Barkal toward a group of burial pyramids to the northwest.

Overleaf:
In the temple of the goddess Mut, one of the principal chambers inside Jebel Barkal, bas-reliefs depict the god Horus (left). A bas-relief still bearing traces of paint (right) depicts the god Amun seated inside the flat-topped mountain. A rock pillar on its east side has been stylized here as the uraeus, or cobra element, of the pharaonic crown.

A full moon accompanied by
Jupiter rises above the royal
necropolis of the southern
capital of the kingdom of Kush
near Bejrawia. The steep-sided
pyramids were built over the
burial chambers of the rulers.

Pyramid and offertory chapel
at the royal necropolis of the
southern capital of the kingdom
of Kush. The pyramids were
infamously plundered by Italian
explorer Giuseppe Ferlini in 1834.

Numbered sections of pillars at the temple of Amun at Naqa, part of the Kushite kingdom, await restoration.

At Musawwarat-es-Sufra, nearby, a bas-relief at the Lion Temple built by King Arnekhamani (c. 235–218 BCE) shows the pharaoh slaughtering captives.

A prehistoric platform tomb
in the Eastern Desert. These
circular burial sites, some of

Overleaf:
Twenty-one days from En Nahud
in Kordofan, this camel train has
already covered about 400 miles

Above and right, now in ruins,
a medieval "castle house," probably from late Christian times
(1250–1450), once guarded the
river at the Dal Cataract, just
above Lake Nasser and the
flooded Second Cataract.

Above, a field of ancient *qubba*—
structures built to hold the
remains of Islamic holy men—
at Old Dongola.

A mud-brick palace from the Christian period overlooks the Nile at Old Dongola. Turned into a mosque in the fourteenth century, it was abandoned in the mid-twentieth century.

Qubbas at El Kabbashi, north of Khartoum, have attracted a field of other graves. The rounded conical form is distinctively Sudanese.

Known since the tenth century, the Red Sea port of Suakin was built largely of coral, which is now rotting in the salt air. Suakin lost its importance when the British built Port Sudan nearby. Restoration has long been proposed, but may now be too late.

Twice prime minister of Sudan, Sadiq al-Mahdi, great-grandson of the Mahdi, leads the Umma Party in Khartoum and is Imam of the Ansar.

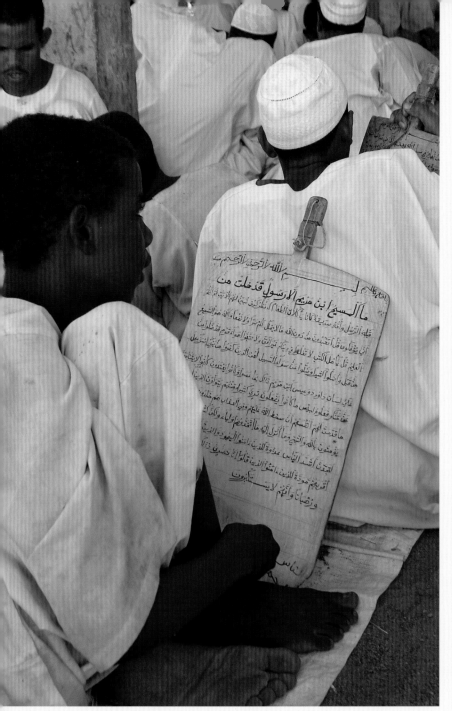

A *khalwa,* or Qur'anic school, at Wad Abu Salih, northeast of Khartoum. The students' time is divided between prayer and study. They recite and memorize texts using wooden tablets prepared daily. During prayer, the head should properly be pressed to the earth, and the boy, center left, has risen with grains of sand still adhering to his forehead.

Prayers at the Khatmiyya mosque
on the eastern edge of Kassala,
the spiritual center for this Sufi
sect in the east of Sudan.

Mahdist forces destroyed
the mosque a year after its
completion, in 1887. Khatmiyya
authorities decreed it should
not be rebuilt.

A leaping Beja sword dance
at Erkowit in the Red Sea Hills.
In the late nineteenth century,
the Beja fought valiantly against
the British and were immortal-
ized in Rudyard Kipling's poem
"Fuzzy-Wuzzy" as "first class
fightin'" men.

A British hill station during the
Condominium period, Erkowit
was a retreat from the heat of
Port Sudan. Its bungalows now
lie in disrepair.

The Shilluk kingdom straddles the White Nile around Malakal. Once dyed a reddish color with brick dust, the togalike cloths worn by men today are commercially produced pink. An elder, above left, has highlighted the traditional scarification across the forehead with a mud paste. Above right, the current *reth* (king) of the Shilluk, a former banker, presides at his rainy-season court in Malakal.

At the local administration office in El Fasher, two *omda* (village headmen) representing sedentary groups, which include the Fur and Zaghawa of rural Darfur, discuss the province's complex issues of violence and population displacement.

Sudan People's Liberation
Movement County Secretary
Mary Biba at work in her office
at Yambio, in the south.

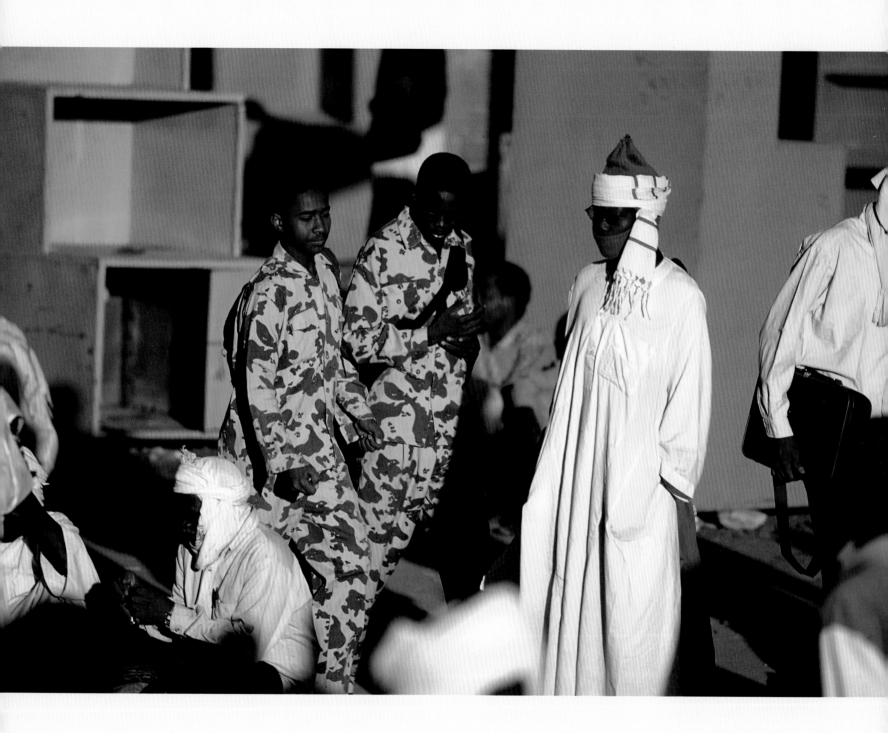

Camouflage cloth is still
commonly used for school
uniforms across the north, a
legacy of militaristic attitudes
during the civil war.

A dance troupe in Yambio, accompanied by a traditional Azande drum and xylophone, acts out the itching caused by sexually transmitted diseases. Sudan People's Liberation Movement authorities use dance as an educational tool for health, economic, and political messages.

Overleaf:
A Kachipo woman on the Boma Plateau, reluctant to wear her *doii*, or lip plate, because of pressure by Sudan People's Liberation Movement authorities to end what they consider to be a harmful traditional practice.

Students in the southern village of Loli on the White Nile learn arithmetic with numbers written in Arabic, a lingua franca across the ethnic groups in the south.

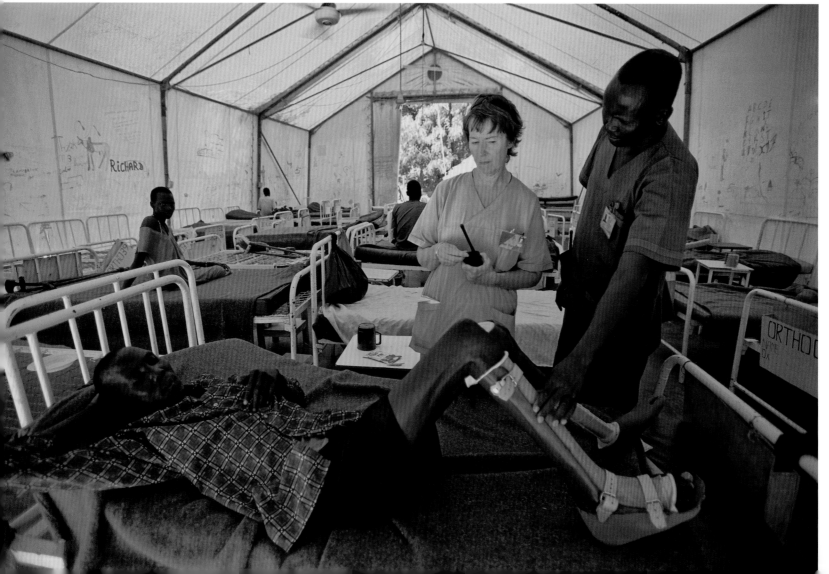

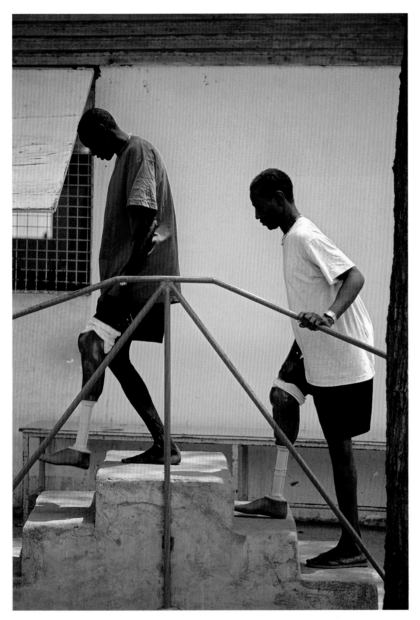

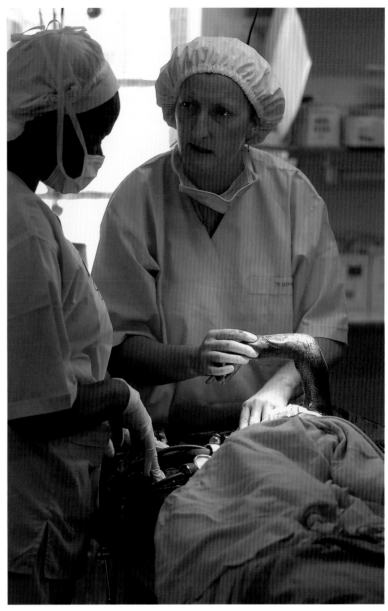

The hospital of the International Committee of the Red Cross at Lopiding, part of the international relief complex centered at Lokichokio in northwest Kenya. The five-hundred-bed hospital has treated the wounded from both rebel and government sides, as well as civilians. Loss of limbs is common among soldiers treated at Lopiding, and prosthetics are designed, manufactured, and fitted there. Above right, surgery on a child in one of the hospital's operating theaters.

Grinding sorghum to make the
staple meal of porridge at the
Jie village of Nawiaporo. The
Kalashnikov assault rifle is for
defense against raiding Toposa
from villages not far away.

At Nzara near Yambio, the 1940s Zande Scheme promoted cotton production, ginning, and textile weaving as a money-earner for the region. A remaining engineer, above, continues to oil and maintain the mill, convinced that the scheme will resume operation with peace.

The government's armed forces in Juba moved damaged armor out of a school compound near the White Nile when they returned the facility to educational use.

Opened in 1979, this camp for
Eritrean refugees is located close
to the border, east of Kassala,
and has by now taken on aspects
of a permanent Sudanese settlement. A young girl, left, fills a
plastic container at one of several
water points in the camp.

Fresh blue tarpaulin shelters at Sereif camp for internally displaced persons, on the outskirts of Nyala, South Darfur.

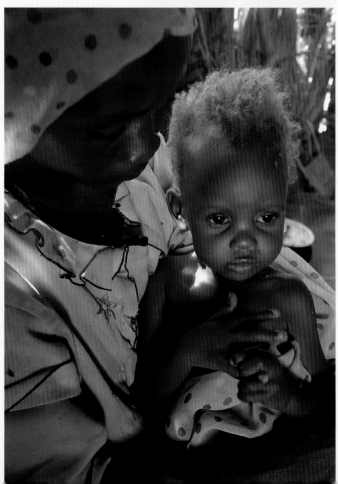

The numbers of internally displaced people across Darfur soared in 2004. The blind woman, opposite, had set up a makeshift shelter on the outskirts of Tawila camp, hoping to receive assistance. The young child, left, in Kalma camp, is suffering from kwashiorkor, a form of protein malnutrition, one symptom of which is a change in hair color. Above, a girl at Abu Shouk camp stirs a sorghum paste for the family meal.

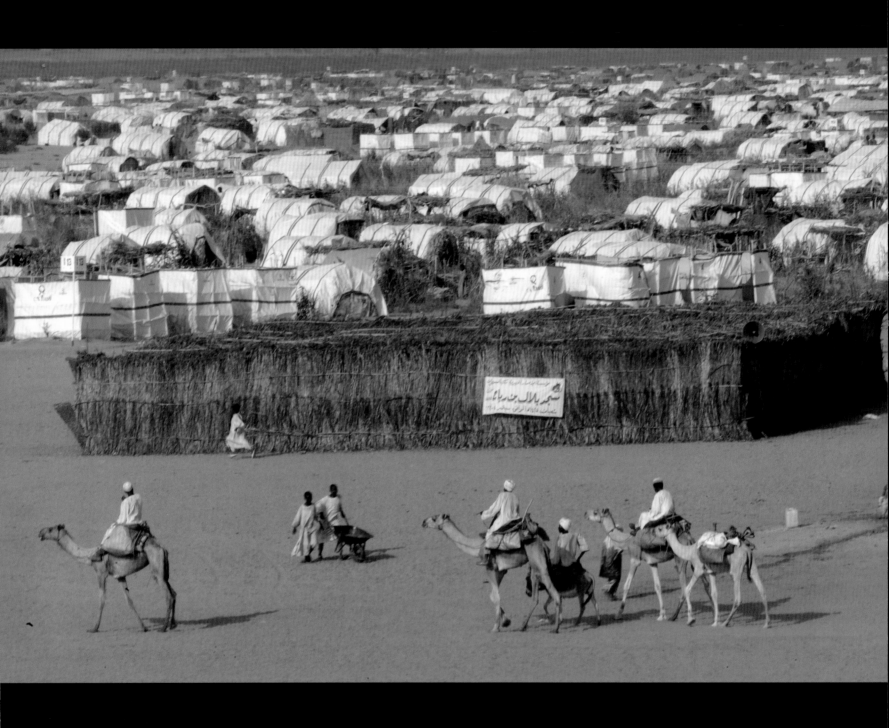

Abu Shouk camp near El Fasher,
north Darfur. The reed enclosure
in front of the encampment is a
mosque, appropriately named
after Bilal, a black slave freed
by the Prophet Muhammad.

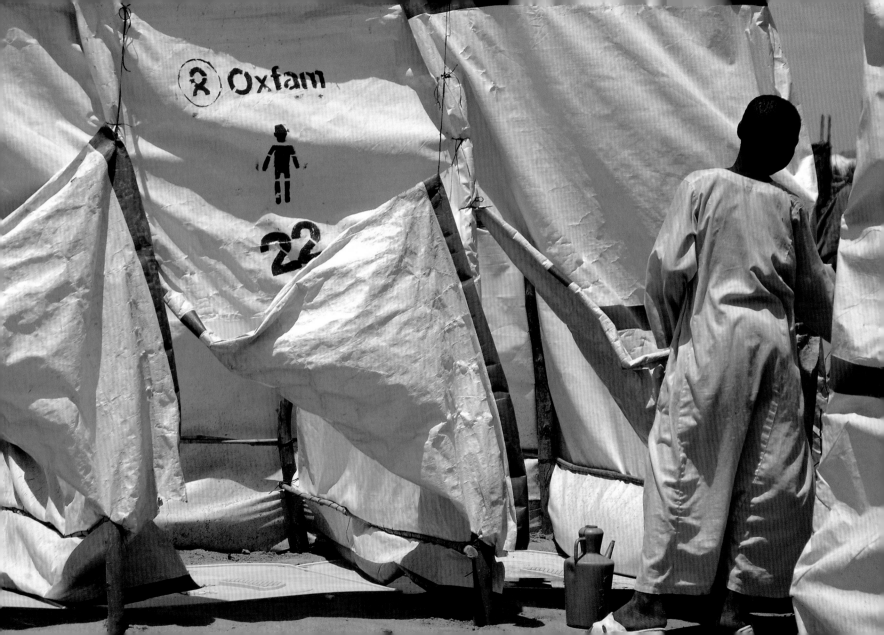

A woman and her daughters, above, newly arrived at Abu Shouk camp on the outskirts of El Fasher, North Darfur.

Primary class under the trees at Zam Zam, another camp for the internally displaced near El Fasher.

Reflective sheeting protects the clinic at Abu Shouk camp from the summer heat.

A Dutch doctor with Samaritan's Purse examines a mother with postnatal complications at Sereif camp, Nyala, South Darfur.

A forty-year-old woman from a village south of El Fasher, recently arrived at Abu Shouk camp after her husband was killed and the village, she said, bombed and burned.

Pro-government demonstration, opposite, in front of the governor's office, El Fasher, September 2004.

Southerners rejoice, above, at the signing of the last two peace protocols, Naivasha, Kenya, December 31, 2004.

93

Above left, Dinka judge and statesman Abel Alier, who advised both delegations in the talks leading up to the peace signed on January 9, 2005, in Nairobi. Earlier, he negotiated the 1972 Addis Ababa Accords that brought a ten-year peace in the civil war.

Above right, Vice-President 'Ali Osman Muhammad Taha, who, with John Garang, leader of the Sudan People's Liberation Movement, negotiated the peace accords ending the civil war between the north and the south.

President ʿUmar al-Bashir and
his defense minister at the
Presidential Palace, Khartoum.

Overleaf:
During Christmas celebrations
in Omdurman, the Coptic bishop,
on the telephone, receives well-
wishers, while the papal nuncio
discusses matters with another
cleric.

Two Mandari boys drink water
through guinea worm filters
supplied by the Carter Center,
whose distribution of millions of
these plastic tubes has reduced
infestations of the debilitating
parasite by 92 percent since 1996.

Oh . . . Nile, You are a descendant of Paradise;
Noble and successful in your destination;
The angels have carried you from the Garden of Eden,
And danced on your luminous waves,
And extended on your banks, green wings.

—from a 1937 poem by Tijani Yusuf Bashir

CHAPTER TWO THE LAND

The folklore, songs, and poems of Sudanese people are suffused with references to the Nile, the world's longest river. The Shilluk, a southern ethnic group, claim that God created a great white cow which emerged from the Nile and gave birth to a man. When this man's grandson married a creature who was half-woman and half-crocodile, she produced Nyikang, the first king of the Shilluk. A northern Arabic ballad gives voice to the widespread sentiment that without the Nile there is no life. No other geographical feature so dominates Sudan's economy, culture, or imagination.

Most of northeastern Africa drains into the Nile River valley, which extends for three thousand miles through the entire length of Sudan and Egypt. Tributaries originating in the hills and mountains of Uganda, the Central African Republic, the Congo, and Ethiopia cross the country to feed the river on its journey to the Mediterranean Sea. The Nile passes from lush forest to swamp, and through savannahs, semiarid plains, rippling sand, and, finally, the bleak rocky desert of the north.

Although most of Sudan sits on an immense plain, it has highlands bordering Ethiopia, Kenya, Uganda, and the Congo. Foothills advance into Ethiopia from the east and north. The Red Sea Hills, an extension of the Ethiopian highlands, separate the northern desert from a narrow coastal strip facing the Red Sea. The Boma Plateau sits on Ethiopia's southwest flank. An extensive ironstone plateau divides the Nile and Congo River watersheds. The Nuba Mountains in central Sudan and the Jebel Marra Mountains in the western region of Darfur provide unique temperate microclimates. Otherwise, the only break in the flatness of the interior terrain comes from assorted *jebels,* large rocky outcrops that stand like isolated sentinels across the plain.

The majority of Sudanese live near the Nile or one of its tributaries. The waters irrigate fields, generate electricity, provide fish, and ferry goods. In the absence of good roads, the Nile has long served as the main commercial artery connecting the south and north. Barges, large and small, carry everything from charcoal, vegetable

Villagers at Um Dalam, north of El Obeid, listen to staff from the International Fund for Agricultural Development, a UN agency, explain how to help forestall desertification.

oil, sugar, and grains to cement and heavy equipment. Villages of daub and wattle *tukuls,* round dwellings made by packing mud onto stalks of sorghum straw, line the banks of the south. The *tukuls* give way to mud-brick houses as the river enters the arid zones. The river connects one ethnic group to another, the villages strung out like African trade beads on a long necklace.

The White Nile

The White Nile leaves Lake Victoria in Uganda and enters Sudan at Nimule. Here in its southern reaches it is called the Bahr al-Jabal, the "mountain river." A hundred miles north of the Ugandan border, it passes Juba, the largest city in the south. Surrounded by grasslands dotted with thorn trees, mangoes, and palms, Juba has been the administrative capital of the south since independence. The long civil war between the north and south has left it largely undeveloped and overcrowded with people displaced by regional conflict.

Throughout most of the south, people east and west of the Nile depend on a combination of cattle herding and subsistence agriculture. Tea, coffee, tobacco, and fruit plantations once thrived in the area and could do so again with peace. The region has forests of teak trees, imported as saplings decades ago, and productive mango orchards planted by colonial administrators and missionaries.

In the settlements of Rumbek, Maridi, Yambio, and Tambura, southerners grow groundnuts (peanuts), cassava, sorghum, and even maize. In Rumbek, the compound of a well-off family includes a large, central thatched hut. Goats are tethered inside overnight. A loft supports massive storage baskets filled with grain, which young women pound into flour with large wooden mortars and long pestles.

Among the Jie at the foot of the Boma Plateau, women and children, including young boys, pound cassava rootstocks into flour. The plateau rises southwest of the border with Ethiopia in an area that includes the 5.6-million-acre (8,799 square miles) Boma National Park. Established in 1981 to protect Africa's largest migrating population of white-eared Kob antelope, Boma had the highest diversity of fauna in Sudan, and perhaps all of Africa, before the civil war. In addition to elephant, hippopotamus, buffalo, and giraffe, the park is home to the eastern black-and-white colobus monkey, whose white fur is used for headdresses by Murle men. Subsistence hunting and cattle raising have put local groups in conflict with wildlife, but the park, one of the largest on the continent, could become an important conservation area with the sustainable use of resources underpinning development efforts.

North of Juba, the river empties into a clay pan that forms the foundation for Africa's largest swamp, the Sudd, which means "barrier" in Arabic. Choked with water hyacinth, reeds, and papyrus, nearly twelve thousand square miles of the Sudd are permanently under water. After the rains, this already vast wetland expands to cover an area three times as large. It proved the biggest obstacle to Egyptian slavers and to early explorers searching for the sources of the Nile and was the bane of later colonial administrators. "The country is only fit for Hippos, mosquitoes, and Nuers to live in. . . . I could not discover the garden of Africa . . . but perhaps it is underneath the Sudd," wrote Colonel J. G. Maxwell, military commander of Egyptian troops in 1899.

As the river works its way through four hundred miles of this tangle of vegetation, it loses half its volume to evaporation and thirsty plants. To this day it remains difficult to find one's way through the swamp. In the early 1980s, traveler John Heminway observed that the Nile sometimes "refused to take a river shape, as in the Sudd, where it spreads across many thousands of miles never quite describing a true riverbank, making travel almost impossible." Still, this vast papyrus-filled basin has attracted some commercial interest. An October 1922 feature on Sudan in *National Geographic* magazine reported that scientists had been "giving attention to the vast papyrus accumulations in the Sudd" with an eye to paper production. Peter Malloy, game warden of the southern Sudan in the early 1950s, noted that an attempt to produce paper was "defeated by the economic impracticability of exporting the product from this heart of desolation." In the 1970s Egypt and Sudan funded the Jonglei project, a scheme to build a canal that would partially drain the Sudd and add precious water to the Aswan Dam. The canal project was suspended in 1983 when civil war between the north and south resumed.

Today's hopes for the swamp center on oil. Geological and seismic surveys completed before 1983 suggest that reserves of at least 1.2 billion barrels lie beneath the Sudd. International oil companies, including TotalElfFina, Petronas, and the China National Petroleum Corporation, have concessionary blocs in the region. With peace, exploration and production in the Sudd could increase Sudan's oil earnings by about $1 billion per year for a decade. The oil sector has already begun looking at the technology needed to overcome the physical challenges posed by the swamp.

No one knows the full extent of Sudan's oil deposits. In addition to the Sudd, the government has granted concessions for exploration in areas including Kordofan, Dinder, eastern Equatoria, the western Upper Nile, Bahr al-Ghazal, Darfur, and eastern Sudan. The Greater Nile Petroleum Operating Company, a consortium that includes Malaysia's Petronas as well as the national oil companies of China and India, has been pumping oil since 1999 from the oil fields north of Bentiu just west of the Sudd. Now producing about 300,000 barrels per day, these fields have an estimated reserve of 1.7 billion barrels. Another consortium, Petrodar Petroleum Operating Company, is scheduled to come onstream in 2005, adding 200,000 barrels a day to the national production.

A thousand-mile-long pipeline carries crude oil from the fields in Unity State to the export terminal on the Red Sea. A parallel line is under construction, and the government has plans to build a third. A new oil refinery north of Khartoum has made Sudan self-sufficient for all its petroleum needs except jet fuel. Most of the rest of the production goes directly to China. Oil is now Sudan's largest source of revenue and is fueling much of the development taking place throughout the country.

Critics have accused the government of forcibly removing local populations from oil-producing areas. The peace accords, which call for the north and south to share oil revenues, will enable the government and local populations to resolve these issues. The oil industry employs tens of thousands of Sudanese from all ethnic groups in the fields, refineries, offices, and ports. It is poised to become the country's single largest employer.

The Bahr al-Ghazal, or Gazelle River, is a major tributary that drains the entire southwest plain and replenishes the Nile before it breaks free of the swamp. The Sobat River, spilling down from the Ethiopian hills, joins the Nile eighty miles later, just south of the port town of Malakal. During the rainy season it is virtually impossible to venture outside of Malakal in even the hardiest vehicle. As a Malakal resident explained, "Upper Nile becomes Upper Mud" for at least half the year.

Sunset turns the smoke from dung fires, lit to protect cattle from mosquitoes and other biting insects, into a rich amber fog near villages along the river. Boran cattle, some magnificent with their huge lyre-shaped horns, are by far the most important possession of most southerners. Owners depend on their cows and bulls for most of life's necessities—from milk and meat to hide, and even urine, which is used as an antiseptic and applied with ash to make insect repellent. Dowries, school fees, and debts are all often paid in cattle.

The harsh climate and difficult geography dictate the rhythm of life for southern cattle herders. During the floods, they must drive their animals to higher ground and away from lethal tsetse flies. The dry season forces them to move the cattle back toward the river and its tributaries. The heavy clay soil, sodden and covered with high grasses during the rainy season, from late April to mid-November, dries with parched cracks under a hot sun the rest of the year.

Wide and sluggish, the White Nile travels more than three hundred miles through a landscape of decreasing vegetation from Malakal to Kosti, a major port linking the north and south, east and west. Acacia forests give way to brush and scrub. A railroad system, begun early in the twentieth century, connects Port Sudan in the northeast to Khartoum, Kassala, Sennar, and Kosti in the center and El Obeid, Nyala, and Wau in the west. The railway bridges the White Nile at Kosti, which sits on a corner of the Gezira (Arabic for "island"), a large, irrigated wedge of land between the White and Blue Niles. Farmers there produce sugar cane, cotton, sorghum, and sesame as well as fruits and vegetables. Steamers and barges originating at Kosti provide the only affordable and reliable transportation to the south. Weary travelers can dine on fresh Nile perch, one of Sudan's finest delicacies, at open-air restaurants on the banks of the river.

The Kenana Sugar Company and its plantation, built in the 1970s, covers more than one hundred square miles on the east bank of the river south of Kosti. Mercurial, derring-do entrepreneurs, both Sudanese and European, sparked this "green gold" project with Louisiana sugar-cane refining technology, hoping to turn Sudan into the region's sugar bowl as well as breadbasket. Kenana produces 400,000 tons of sugar a year, of which 100,000 tons are exported.

Harvesting cane requires teamwork. Carefully watching the wind, a team fires the section to be cut. The leaves burn off quickly with a light charring of parts of the stalk. The heat concentrates the sugar—and chases snakes from the field. Before dawn the cutters arrive, flashlights strapped to their heads and machetes swinging. As piles of cane mount, specially designed trucks arrive to haul the harvest to the plant for processing.

Durra market in the center
of Khartoum, c. 1920s.
Sudan Times Postcard Series

Kenana is a metaphor for the possibilities of modern Sudan. With more than eighty-five hundred permanent staff and thousands of additional seasonal employees it has given birth to a small town with a population of more than thirty thousand from every region of the country. Two dozen primary schools and six secondary schools educate the workers' children. The town, planned by architects and engineers, has a hospital and provides basic services including running water, sewage, and electricity.

The Blue Nile

The Blue Nile, a swift, beautiful river, pours out of the Ethiopian highlands, falling 4,600 feet from Lake Tana through a series of cataracts on its 975-mile journey to Khartoum. It carries seven times as much water as the White Nile during the main runoff between July and October, causing floods all along its banks. The river leaves the Ethiopian mountains at the border village of Bumbodi and passes quickly into Sudan through Fazughli, renowned for its gold mines in the early nineteenth century.

The river rushes on to Roseires, site of the country's most recent dam, built in the 1960s with World Bank money to compensate Sudan for the flooding caused by construction of the Aswan Dam. The hydroelectric turbines at Roseires generate much of Sudan's electric power, and the dam's spillway gates regulate, to a degree, the flow of the Blue Nile.

The Blue Nile cuts through hot, flat plains to Sennar, the former capital of the Funj kingdom. At the height of their power, the Funj ruled an area that extended west beyond the White Nile and north almost to the border with Egypt. Jacques Charles Poncet, a French doctor and explorer who visited Sennar in 1699, described a thriving city with a population of nearly one hundred thousand, its women richly attired in silk and silver jewelry. At that time, Sennar traded extensively with India through the Red Sea port of Suakin. A huge market offered everything from slaves and ivory to tamarind fruit, gold dust, and tobacco. It was also a major trading center for horses and camels. Theodor Krump, a Bavarian missionary who stopped in Sennar in 1701, reported that the central square was "as big as that of Munich." Sennar is today a dusty town distinguished by wide streets, a railroad station, a market, and an important dam. Its economy, like that of most of Sudan, depends largely on farming.

In an early effort to support agriculture in Sudan, the Anglo-Egyptian Condominium government built major dams along the Nile. The first two projects, completed in the 1920s at Jebel Aulia and Sennar, dammed the White and Blue Niles respectively and enabled the irrigation of the Gezira Peninsula between the rivers. Silt deposits have ended the usefulness of the Jebel Aulia Dam, but the Sennar Dam continues to irrigate 2.1 million acres in the Gezira.

Developed by the British during the colonial period, the Gezira scheme began as a unique consortium of government, farmers, and commercial interests to produce cotton and vegetables. Sir James Robertson, the Condominium's last civil secretary, noted that until the mid-1940s Sudan as a whole largely depended on the scheme for both its revenue and food. Today, one hundred thousand farmers work plots of up to thirty *feddan* (roughly thirty acres) and still produce much of the food for the north. The diet throughout Sudan depends on two grains, millet and sorghum, or *dukhun* and *durra,* both of which are strongly drought resistant. *Durra* is grown on nearly half the cultivated land in the country. The Gezira pro-duces the largest crop, but nearly every rural family, be they in the far west of Darfur, the Nuba Mountains, or the southern states, plants a small patch of millet or sorghum for making porridge and bread.

Not so long ago, cotton grown in the Gezira accounted for more than half of Sudan's export earnings. The high-est quality cotton is long-fiber Egyptian cotton, much of which is exported to Europe. The crop is much smaller now, fallen to 5 percent of its greatest production, thanks in large part to competition from China with its cheap syn-thetic textiles. One cotton farmer might plant ten *feddan* each in cotton and sorghum, and leave ten fallow. Cotton yields are good, thirty-six *guntar* (one *guntar* equals about one hundred pounds) for four *feddan*. As a member of the modern Gezira scheme, the farmer covers production costs with a loan, which he reimburses to the organization in cotton at the end of the harvest.

Near Wad Medani, two tributaries, the Dinder and the Rahad, empty into the Blue Nile from the east during the rains and then dry up by December or January. Both riv-ers cut through the 2.2-million-acre (3,459 square miles) Dinder National Park, the only surviving tract of woodland and flood plain in the country's vast savannah grasslands zone. Established in 1935, the park encompasses three distinct ecosystems and houses twenty-seven species of large mammals. Located on a major north-south migratory flyway, the park supports 250 species of birds. Recogniz-ing that protecting this park is of global importance, the United Nations Development Program, together with the Global Environment Facility and the Food and Agricultural Organization, are working with the government of Sudan and local communities to develop a management plan that would preserve the area's biodiversity and provide for the sustainable use of its resources.

Khartoum

From the air above Khartoum, the two rivers that form the main Nile look like long snakes, one a milk chocolate color and the other darker; sometimes during winter and in the right light, it is almost a midnight blue. The White Nile slithers from the south, and the Blue Nile tumbles in from the east. Each is fringed in a crazy-quilt pattern of green and brown fields that peter out into a desert that stretches to the horizon. The "white" and "blue" rivers col-lide in Khartoum, their colors mixing in the Mughran, the confluence of the Nile. Neither gives up its identity easily, and a distinct dividing line extends for hundreds of yards

toward Omdurman until the two unite, moving north to Egypt as the Nile.

For nearly two centuries people from different ethnic groups have gravitated to Khartoum and, like the rivers, collided and blended. Young and old dressed in both indig-enous and modern clothing crowd the streets. Men, some in turbans and *jelabia*, others in suits and ties, dash along-side each other into office buildings. Northern women can usually be distinguished by their colorful *tobes* and south-ern women by their more form-fitting batiks.

Greater Khartoum actually encompasses three quite different cities. Khartoum, post-Mahdia colonial adminis-trative city and seat of government, sits on the peninsula between the Blue and White Niles. Huge mahogany trees along the Corniche, called simply Nile Avenue, protect the bank in front of the presidential palace. Omdurman, a more traditional Sudanese town with mud-brick houses and inner courtyards, grew up on the left bank of the main Nile just north of the Mughran. The Omdurman *suq*, or market, open seven days a week, is a maze of alleys with shops offering every conceivable merchandise: antique swords from the Mahdia period; old African trade beads; brand-new gold bangles from the Gulf States; Persian rugs brought back from the hajj, the pilgrimage to Mecca; and textiles from China. Foreign residents, including a growing number of European and Asian businessmen, often visit on the Friday holiday, when it is less crowded.

Industrial development has taken place in Khartoum North, the newest settlement. Some of the city's most beautiful homes are found here on the banks of the Blue Nile. Today perhaps as many as eight or nine million people, including some three million southerners who have been displaced by the war, live in the greater Khartoum region.

In the capital, modern industry mingles with the tradi-tional. One of the world's most sophisticated Coca-Cola plants stands cheek by jowl with small factories churning out everything from edible oils and dried fruits to foot-wear, textiles, and cosmetics, including henna for hair and body decoration. Steel silos and wheat processing plants tower over small family-run bakeries. Pharmaceutical fac-tories, large and small, produce a wide range of generic drugs, including aspirin and cold medicines as well as specialized antibiotics and antimalarials. Light industry accounts for more than 20 percent of the country's gross domestic product, up from just 10 percent in 1997.

The automobile maker GIAD, whose name is drawn from the Arabic word for "horses," assembles cars and pickups to compete with Japanese and European sports cars, trucks, and buses. Subsidiaries of Caterpillar and John Deere vie for customers. Mobitel, a joint venture between the government and private industry, operates one of the most profitable cell phone networks in Africa, with more than one million subscribers. International oil companies, including Petronas, China National Petroleum Corporation, and the Indian Oil and Natural Gas Corporation, have large administrative offices in Khartoum. Their investments have spurred the growth of new service industries that are employing tens of thousands of people and significantly broadening Sudan's middle class.

Suq Libya, a large sprawling market area north of Omdurman, sells livestock as well as food and household supplies. Goats, sheep, cattle, and camels are on offer. Camels, an important Sudanese export, are not just for transport or eating. Those from Sudan are reputed to be the best racing camels in the Middle East, and it is not surprising to find Gulf State *shaykhs* on hand for trial races. Boy jockeys, only seven or eight years old, are strapped onto camels that show their mettle in spirited heats before potential buyers.

The Nile

The united Nile leaves Khartoum and heads straight north to the closest of the six major cataracts between the

capital and the Egyptian border. An American adventurer, Bayard Taylor, who spent twenty-six days sailing up the Nile in the mid-nineteenth century, described the narrowing of the river between high hills of naked red sandstone rock at the Sabaluqa gorge, or Sixth Cataract. "At sunset we were completely shut in the savage solitude," he noted, "and there we seemed likely to remain, for the wind came from all quarters by turns, and jammed the vessel against the rocks more than once." A hundred and fifty years later, the American traveler Paul Theroux described a calmer vista: "All I saw was a series of muddy rapids that were easily navigable in a small boat. We made camp in a grove of trees under which were several rope beds." Theroux thought the spot was idyllic but "so marginalized and so self-sufficient that nothing will change it." The gorge remains a scene of beauty but no longer of solitude. Much frequented by newly affluent day trippers from the capital, it has become an especially favorite spot on holidays, complete with traffic jams on the desert bank.

About one hundred miles north of Khartoum, the Nile passes Shendi, once one of the country's main crossroads. Historically the town sat on the Nile at a spot known as The Gates, just where the river is closest to the southern end of the Red Sea, at the edge of the rainbelt south of the Sahara. The east-west caravan routes converged here on their journeys elsewhere.

John Lewis Burkhardt, an Arabic-speaking Swiss scholar turned explorer, spent a month in Shendi in 1814. He found a small town with a huge market that seemed to be in the middle of nowhere. Every Friday and Saturday, merchants opened small stalls and sold spices and sandalwood from India, swords and razors from Germany, beads and writing paper from Italy, cloth, pottery, and soap from Egypt, saddles and other leather goods from Kordofan, and Ethiopian gold. A large livestock market drew distant buyers for the famed Dongola horses as well as for camels and donkeys needed to carry goods across the desert. Traders, including the palest Arabs and the blackest Africans, came from all over Sudan. Those coming from the Red Sea exchanged Indian goods for gold, horses, and slaves. "Commerce," wrote Burkhardt, "was the very life of society." He estimated that five thousand slaves, taken from every ethnic group along the Nile, passed through the Shendi market every year, noting that Muslim traders circumcised young boys purchased as slaves and immediately gave them Arab names. Shendi remains a busy market town that draws international traffic today thanks primarily to the nearby pyramids at Bejrawia, also called Meroe.

Antipoaching efforts are challenged by new raw ivory available in the Rumbek market, left, and by finished ivory and even rhino horn in Omdurman.
Photo: Timothy Carney

This region is also known for its iron ore. Sudan's long history of working iron dates to the days of the kingdom of Kush. Early Western travelers compared Meroe with industrial Britain and dubbed it the Birmingham of the South. Quantities of ferrous silicate ore are underfoot near the pyramids, and slag piles are found not far away. Sudan has additional, largely unexploited, iron-ore deposits in the south, west, and Red Sea hills. Despite these reserves, the country imports all its steel for light industries.

Just north of Shendi, the seasonal Atbara River, the last tributary, joins the Nile. The great river proceeds for another 150 miles and at Abu Hamad bends southwest to the Fourth Cataract, where a new dam is being built to generate hydroelectric power as well as provide irrigation for the surrounding area. The Merowe Dam, named after the small island in the river and not to be confused with the pyramids, will create a lake nearly three miles wide and extending more than one hundred miles south along the river. New government-built villages will accommodate the forty-eight thousand people displaced by the dam. Government plans include a large agricultural scheme that would inject wealth into this desperately poor region. There is, however, grave concern that the project will drown important archaeological sites just as the High Dam of Aswan did in northern Nubia. Archaelogical teams are busy surveying the area. Located between the Fourth Cataract and Dongola are several important archaeological sites once part of the Napata capital of the Kushite kingdom, including Jebel Barkal, Nuri, and El Kurru. At Old Dongola, the river turns north again, a muddy ribbon nourishing a ruffle of green along its banks.

Stark desert, stretching as far as the eye can see and beyond, flanks the Nile in the north. The bleak landscape of rock and sand, carved by millennia of wind and water erosion, provides a dramatic backdrop to nomad tents and camel caravans on their way to trading outposts along the Egyptian border and the Red Sea. Nomads, following centuries-old trade routes, herd their camels north, occasionally crossing the black lines of a modern asphalt highway.

The tarred road, however, ends on the west bank of the Nile at Dongola, a town pushing slowly into the modern era with phone cards for public telephones. Visitors to the north must have sturdy four-wheel-drive vehicles equipped with extra water and gasoline as well as the perforated steel planks that are vital for getting out of soft sand. In this, one of the country's poorest and least

developed regions, there are no hotels and few amenities. Travelers either sleep under the stars in the desert or as guests in the extremely modest, but interestingly painted homes of Nubian families.

The *suq* in Omdurman, c. 1920s. Sudan Times Postcard Series

The Eastern Desert and Port Sudan

To the east of the Nile lies the Nubian Desert, a source of gold for the Egyptian pharaohs. A celebrated inscription from the reign of Ramses II (1270–1212 BCE) describes the difficulty of extracting the precious metal: "Only half the men of the gold washers arrived because others died of thirst on the way, as indeed did the donkeys whom they led with them." This parched world of boulders and rocky outcroppings is yielding its gold a little more easily today.

Large-scale gold production began in 1991 under an agreement between the Sudanese government and a French agency that created the Ariab Mining Company. Ariab's open pit lies just ten miles from one of the pharaonic mines, but the ancients could not have exploited a site like Ariab, whose silica-barite ore requires a complex chemical extraction process before smelting. The mine moves sixty million tons of rock annually which eventually reduces to five tons of gold. The gold ingots poured at Ariab are, in fact, the ancient metal electrum, which contains more than 20 percent silver.

Like all major companies in Sudan today, Ariab employs a mix of people from all regions of the country. It created the nearby village of Bir Ajam to house the nine hundred families of workers brought to the desolate area. In addition to providing housing, the company subsidizes three schools, and a clinic. It pays the salaries of a doctor and a nurse. Ariab is not alone in this. The government insists that all foreign companies investing in Sudan include community development projects in education and health as part of their business plans.

In addition to gold, Sudan has commercially viable quantities of silver, chromium, mica, and gypsum. Southeastern Sudan has more than a million tons of largely untapped chromite reserves. Some 250 million tons of gypsum are located in the vicinity of Khartoum and the Red Sea coast.

Port Sudan, the country's main port on the Red Sea, handles about five million tons of cargo per year and has been recently expanded. Its thirteen berths and fifteen silos hold grain, cotton, gum arabic, and sesame. The Chinese have added facilities for bulk cargo, including wheat, now a major import as Sudanese have turned to wheat-based bread as a staple in their diet. South of the main port, Chinese contractors have also built a new terminal for oil products that can accommodate fifty-thousand-ton ships.

In 1994, the Cousteau Society, in conjunction with UNESCO, completed the first survey of the Red Sea since Cousteau's 1953 film *The World without Sun*. Cousteau did most of his research for that production from a base at Shab Rumi, thirty miles north of Port Sudan. The submarine dock is still there, now completely covered with coral. The society is working with the Sudanese government to establish an ongoing program based in Port Sudan that would support the sustainable development of the Red Sea and its resources.

Sudan's Red Sea coastline stretches more than four hundred miles, but the Sudanese have done little to exploit the sea's bounty. For the most part, Sudanese fishermen still follow traditional ways. They set out in small boats and bring their catch back to the Port Sudan markets in the early morning. A joint German-Sudanese venture, however, would establish a cannery to process forty thousand tons of tuna annually, a factory to process thirty thousand tons of shrimp per year, and a fish-meal plant.

Kassala

Travelers driving south from Port Sudan pass through the rocky ridges of the Red Sea Hills and semiarid flatlands before reaching the town of Kassala. Here fertile lands, seasonally watered by the Gash River as it flows out of Eritrea after the rains, produce an abundance of fruit and vegetables. There is an old saying that he who drinks from the Nile will return to Sudan. In fact, anyone who has tasted a Sudanese grapefruit—especially one grown around Kassala—will want to come back for more.

The town's main market offers mountains of grapefruit, oranges, and limes as well as tomatoes, eggplant, carrots, onions, and cucumbers. One of the biggest sorghum harvests comes from the rich agricultural area between Kassala and the town of Qadarif. Plots of sorghum extend from the highways like the corn fields of the midwestern United States.

The Western Desert, Darfur, and Kordofan

The Libyan Desert, lying west of the Nile, is only slightly more hospitable than the Nubian Desert. There are no permanent settlements in the far north, although camel nomads continue to depend on a few natural water holes as well as man-made wells.

Natural climatic changes, population pressures, and overgrazing are accelerating desertification throughout western Sudan. The Sahara has been creeping east and south from Darfur into Kordofan at the rate of about three miles a year for the last five decades. Grayish red sands now cover thousands of square miles of once tillable land. The stumpy trees used for poles and firewood are fast disappearing, and many of the shallow dry-season wells that could once be dug out by hand are gone.

In 1996 the University of Khartoum created the Institute for Desertification and Desert Cultivation. Some researchers have argued that climate change, not human abuse, is the real villain in land degradation. Sudan's Agricultural Research Corporation, however, says that half the country's twenty-six states are suffering serious environmental degradation, and excessive pressure from humans and livestock on limited resources has combined with recurrent drought cycles to produce a dangerous situation. This is clear in villages like Um Dalam in Kordofan. Encroaching sand dunes threaten to engulf the area, and may soon force the village to relocate. The International Fund for Agricultural Development, a specialized United Nations agency, has been working with villagers to adopt agricultural and animal husbandry practices to stem the advance of the desert, but it may be too late.

Ground water has always been the country's most precious natural resource in areas removed from the Nile. Some still-functioning Nubian wells, dating to the Meroitic pre-Christian period, are at least two thousand years old. In Kordofan and Darfur, both man and beast depend on ancient wells and modern bore holes. Herders, many still using old leather goatskins, painstakingly haul water up for their cattle, sheep, goats, and camels from century-old holes sunk as deep as one hundred yards.

Some of the country's most important aquifers are found in formations in and around the central province of Kordofan, in a large area around Khartoum, under the Gash River near Kassala on the Eritrean border, and by Port Sudan on the Red Sea coast. People and their animals, however, are inexorably lowering the water table in all Sudan's semiarid regions, bringing farmers and pastoralists into greater conflict in the marginal areas of Darfur and Kordofan.

In the west, as in the south, many people count their wealth in livestock, be it camels, cattle, sheep, or goats. Camels, much sought after for both meat and transport by Egypt and the Gulf States, have long been a major source of income for nomads across the northern reaches of the country.

The majority of Sudanese farmers in Kordofan and Darfur practice subsistence agriculture. In the early fall of 2004, fields of millet covered much of the 125 square miles between El Fasher and Tawila in north Darfur. The crop, however, did not look especially rich, a poor harvest adding to the burden of people in that strife-torn region.

The west, however, produces gum arabic, one of the country's most important exports. The knobby, amber-colored resin exuded from the *Acacia senegal,* an unprepossessing tree called *hashab* in Arabic, is a key ingredient in diverse products ranging from chewing gum to fertilizers and explosives. Ground into a powder, gum arabic helps create the foam in beer, the chewiness in gumdrops, and the smoothness in ice cream. It is used in rubber making, leather tanning, cosmetics, and pharmaceuticals. Sudan produces three-fifths of the world's supply. Gum arabic is so important to western industry that the United States exempted it from the economic sanctions it imposed on Sudan in 1997.

Although most gum arabic comes from Kordofan province, the *hashab* tree is found all across the central semiarid belt in Sudan. Trees grow wild, but by common understanding families inherit rights to them and camp nearby during the harvesting season. Sudanese also cultivate *hashab* trees in gum gardens on land that would otherwise stand fallow after five years of growing other crops such as sorghum, melons, peanuts, or sesame. Farmers score the branches of the *hashab* trees late in the year. The resin, "the first child of the tree," is swept off after a month or so. The second exudation produces blobs of gum arabic that are sometimes as large as tennis balls. It is picked, dried, and bagged in hundred-pound lots.

Sudan has two major auction houses for gum arabic and other agricultural products. One is in El Obeid, the capital of Kordofan state. The other is in Qadarif, the commercial center of the state of Qadarif, southeast of Khartoum. The Qadarif auctioneer whistled down one lot of gum arabic in January 2004 at US$0.36 per pound. Both powder and crystals are produced for export.

This central region also supplies sesame for local consumption and for export to neighboring countries, having replaced cotton as Sudan's primary agricultural export. A major plant in El Obeid crushes the seeds to produce sesame oil for market. Smaller, family-run operations can still be found scattered across the province. At one, founded in 1926, a blindfolded camel pulls a pestle around a large, wooden mortar, grinding one bag of sesame a day. The camel survives two years; the mortar and pestle last, at best, three. An Arab proverb describes a narrow-minded man as a "camel grinding sesame."

South of El Obeid in the Nuba Mountains, hillside fields yield millet, an ancient grain and staple that northern Sudanese believe gives men the energy to do hard work. Farmers in this area also grow the red-blossomed hibiscus flowers that, when dried, produce a cranberry-colored tea, *karkade,* a staple of every Sudanese kitchen that is also exported to neighboring countries.

In addition to *karkade,* both southerners and northerners drink copious quantities of tea and coffee. The Hadendowa of eastern Sudan always consume a prime number of small cups of coffee—prime to show the unity of Allah. Usually made by attractive women to draw in the male clientele, the Sudanese version of Turkish coffee, thick and flavored with cardamom, ginger, and cloves, is available everywhere, from the tree-shaded market in Rumbek to the roadside stalls in the Nuba Mountains to the northern town of Kerma. In the morning, up and down the Nile, it goes well with *zelabia,* a delicious, deep-fried beignet sprinkled with sugar.

The Nile and its tributaries are a uniting force, linking one region to another. Its waters are Sudan's most precious natural resource. Water and its availability dictate what crops can be grown and where livestock can be pastured. The ebb and flow of the rivers influence the economics and culture of the majority of the population.

Overleaf:
In its middle reaches, the White Nile meanders sluggishly north of Bor through the Sudd—the world's largest marshland.

A Nuer canoe crosses the White Nile to the port town of Malakal just before nightfall.

Azande children carry honey through the grass near Maridi, close to the border with the Congo.

Overleaf:
A granite boulder in the Red Sea Hills, left in precarious balance as erosion cut away the sandy ground in which it was embedded.

The wind-sculpted ridge of a huge *barkhan* (dune) casts its shadow on its steep inner face, south of Old Dongola in the Nubian Desert.

White-eared Kob antelope (*Kobus leucotis*) near the Boma Plateau in April, at the beginning of their migration to follow the rains beginning to fall to the southwest.

Opposite, flocks of white pelican
(*Pelecanus onocrotalus*) on a
lake in Dinder National Park,
close to the Blue Nile.

Above, greater flamingos
(*Phoenicopterus ruber*) on
the White Nile just above
Omdurman.

Left, a pink-backed pelican
(*Pelecanus rufescens*) on
the White Nile near Malakal.

The Boma Plateau rises above the Nile's floodplain in the southeast, bordering Ethiopia. Old volcanic plugs dot the landscape, the nearest carrying the Murle name Ngatiloni

A massive baobab (*Adansonia digitata*) in Kordofan, at the tail end of a dust storm.

Hollowed out and filled with water in the rains, baobabs act as village storage tanks through the long dry season. British forces secured a chain of filled baobab for their water supply during the 1916 campaign against the independent sultanate of Darfur.

Nomads near the Meroitic ruins
of Musawwarat use a donkey to
draw goatskins of water from a
well and fill plastic containers.

In the village of Bir Ajam in the
Red Sea Hills, a foot-pumped well
is one of a series dug by the Ariab
gold mine for the communities
that supply its workers.

The "Greek well" in the city of
El Obeid, capital of Kordofan,
was named after the merchant
who had it dug to water his
herds of cattle.

Householders fill jars with water
for passersby in Abu Fatima
village in Nubia, where rainfall
is negligible.

The Gezira, between the White
and Blue Niles south of Khartoum, is the country's most fertile
agricultural area. Irrigated since
the 1920s, it produces a large
variety of crops, including cotton,
here piled into large mounds to
be weighed and packed.

Most of Sudan's sugar production is concentrated at Kenana, in the Gezira. As the dawn signals the end of his shift, a southern *katakau*, or canecutter, slices through blackened stalks following controlled burning the night before. Sacks of refined sugar are loaded by conveyor belt to waiting trucks.

A type of sandstorm unique to the region, the *haboob* forms within minutes as huge downdrafts of air in storm clouds force dust and sand outward. On a January afternoon, the wall of a *haboob* advances toward a livestock market in Omdurman, soon engulfing it in swirling brick-red grit.

A fisherman on the White Nile near Malakal.

Overleaf:
A Nuer family paddles through the backwaters of the White Nile to Malakal, their canoe loaded with thatch and firewood.

The Blue Nile rises in the highlands of Ethiopia. Fishing from the shore near Khartoum, at left, and above, sandbanks north of Sennar.

A riverside village under palms, in
the lush riverine lands bordering
the White Nile near Malakal.

Dal village, close by the Nile
cataract of the same name, sits
in a barren landscape of granite
boulders and sand, typical of
the northern Nubian Desert.

South of Juba, during the Christmas season a Latuka girl paints the walls of the family *tukul*, the circular mud-plastered dwelling with conical thatched roof typical of the region.

In Nubia, mineral pigments are crushed from local rock and dissolved in water for painting. Although the colors will eventually fade in the fierce sunlight, there is almost no rain to make them run.

The seasonal painting of Nubian houses in the north is the responsibility of women, who choose the designs and colors.

A massive kiln, sited on clay deposits, fires bricks on the outskirts of El Fasher in Darfur.

Making bricks from the
abundant clay along the
Blue Nile at Khartoum.

The Ariab gold mines in the Red
Sea Hills, operated since 1991 as
a joint venture between a French
company and the government.
The huge open-pit mines begin
with blasting and end, after a few
years of extraction, with tailings
stained green with copper
precipitates.

Once gold has been extracted by heap leaching, 26-kilo ingots are poured, the slag hammered off, and the Ariab Mining Company's identifying marks stamped. The

Oil production is concentrated at Heglig, south of the Nuba Mountains. On a Chinese drilling rig at Simbir West -3, above, workers add a new section of pipe. The well, already 2354 meters deep after twelve days of drilling, may go as far as 3660 meters (11,000 feet). At the central processing facility, opposite, crude oil is drawn for sampling before beginning its 1000-mile journey along the pipeline to Port Sudan.

Overleaf:
One of two main oil storage tanks at the central processing facility, each with a capacity of 300,000 barrels of crude.

Gathering sea salt at a salt evaporation pond south of Port Sudan.

A woman winnows sorghum,
harvested from the plot around
her house in the western Nuba
Mountains.

The December sorghum harvest near Qadarif. Almost half the cultivated land in Sudan is given over to the crop.

Huge woven baskets store
sorghum in a granary loft
in Rumbek.

At Saad Nefenty village,
Nubia, dates are stored in
large terracotta jars (*gosieba*)
that are sealed with plaster
and whitewashed.

Baking bread in outdoor ovens at Dudia on the road west of El Obeid.

A livestock trader carrying a watermelon at Suq Libya, Omdurman.

Palm oil for sale in Yambio
market.

Harvesting groundnuts in July
near Maridi.

Preparing onions at the *suq*
in Omdurman.

Sudan produces 60 percent of
the world's supply of gum arabic,
the resin of several acacia trees,
principally *Acacia senegal*. An
emulsifier and thickening agent
used in foods, adhesives, and
inks, it is a major export for the

Harvesting the hibiscus variety whose petals produce *karkade*, a red, slightly astringent infusion that is immensely popular in Sudan and throughout the Middle East. This crop will be auctioned in El Obeid.

With one of the most modern plants in the world, Khartoum's Coca-Cola company provides equal job opportunity, in this case by hiring deaf women to inspect bottles.

A Dinka man relaxes with a pipe at Rumbek market, where tobacco is sold around a huge old tree.

On the Boma Plateau, an elderly Murle woman draws on a homemade water-pipe fashioned from a gourd.

At a coffee shop frequented by
Beja men in Port Sudan, Egyptian
glass water-pipes, or *shisha*,
provide a shared, cool smoke.

El Obeid has a modern factory that crushes oil from sesame. But this family business dates to 1926, and since then one camel after another has ground a bag of sesame a day, producing oil for sale in the neighborhood and at the market. The sesame cake waste makes good fodder.

A scuba diving boat and container ships share the harbor at Port Sudan, the country's sole trading outlet on the Red Sea.

Stevedores load a Red Sea coastal freighter at the port with bags of sesame for export to Yemen and Egypt.

A raft woven from bundles of
reeds carries a load of charcoal
downriver to Malakal, where the
two Nuer men, after a forty-hour
voyage, hope to sell it.

Canoes laden with goods for
market are paddled upriver
on the White Nile.

Loading a truck at a stop during
the long journey from the west to
Khartoum. The painted pierced-
steel plank, or PSP, on the side
of the truck is wedged under the
wheels to extricate the vehicle
from deep sands.

Imported textiles at the
Omdurman *suq*.

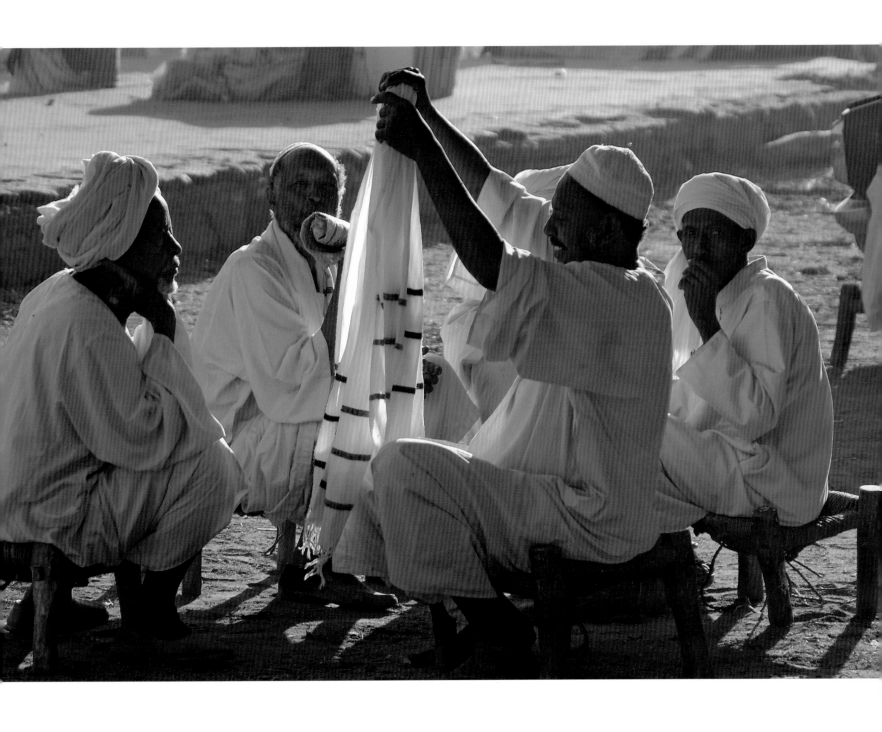

Examining a shawl at Kassala's fruit and vegetable market.

Overleaf:
A traditional and typical *gahawa*, or coffee shop, in the shade of a tree at Kassala.

A stall selling mobile phones at Suq Libya, Omdurman.

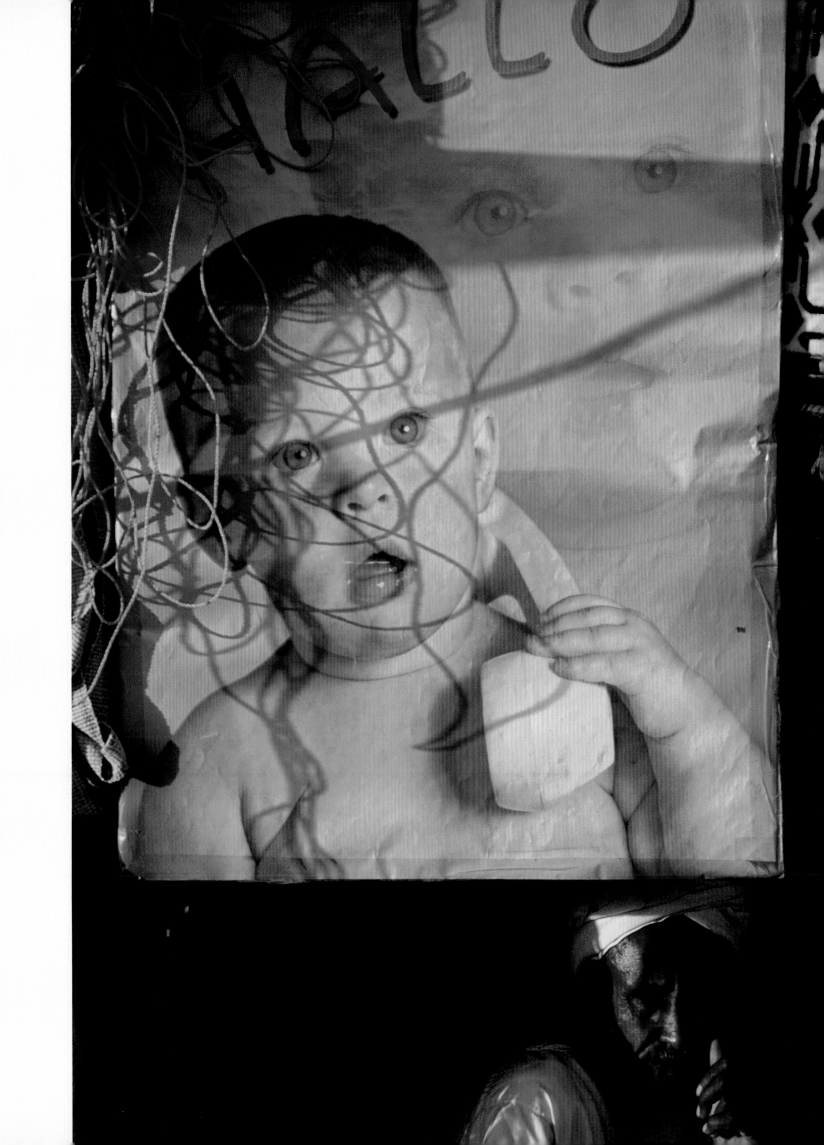

A roadside merchant at Suq
Libya, Omdurman.

Roofing thatch for sale at the
market in Tawila, Darfur.

Boran cattle, the wealth and
pride of their owners, stroll
through a Dinka cattle camp
north of Rumbek. Smoldering
dried cow dung protects against
insects.

Milk for sale in large gourd bowls
at the *suq* in El Fasher.

Cattle returning to a riverside
village near Malakal on the
White Nile.

A herdsman moves cattle toward
market east of Kassala.

Two weeks before camel races
are staged for potential buyers,
many of them from Saudi Arabia,
a series of heats takes place in the
desert north of Omdurman. Young
boy jockeys are strapped into the
saddles of the racing camels.

Chase cars give encouragement
and lend a helping hand, as
necessary.

Herding camels in the western
Nuba Mountains.

Arabian thoroughbreds exercise along the Blue Nile in the early morning.

The Sixth Cataract at Sabaluqa, the uppermost of the rapids on the Nile and the closest to Khartoum.

The Presidential Palace, Khartoum, on the banks of the Blue Nile close to its junction with the White Nile. This building, above, replaced the original razed in 1885 by the Mahdi's forces after Governor-General Charles Gordon had been killed on its steps.

At the western edge of the Bayud
Desert, southwest of the great
bend on the Nile and the Fourth
Cataract.

Desiccated "desert melons"
(*Citrullus colocynthis*) in the
Nubian Desert east of the Nile,
between the Fourth and Third
Cataracts.

Camels perish regularly on the
long journey north to Egypt.

CHAPTER THREE   THE PEOPLE

Sudan owes its unrivaled diversity to its long history as a major economic crossroads for Africa, the Middle East, and the Mediterranean. Ancient trade routes linking West Africa to the Arabian Peninsula and to the Egyptian coast all passed through Sudan. Here, for thousands of years, disparate cultures—African, Egyptian, Greek, Turk, and Arab—have collided and blended to produce people of great beauty who share a turbulent history and rich heritage. Their society since the earliest times has been in flux, as it is today.

Observers often describe Sudan as ethnically divided between the Arab Muslim north and the African south, where traditional religions predominate. This broad characterization does not begin to convey the social complexity within these regions or the degree to which different ethnic groups have influenced customs across regions, producing a unique Afro-Arab culture. Arabs and Africans alike divide themselves into specifically named ethnic groups, and in every area of the country these ethnic groups subsist as either nomadic herders or sedentary farmers. Much of the intergroup conflict in the south, west, and east results from competition over resources.

In a trend that has accelerated over the last two decades, nomads are becoming more sedentary, their traditions eroded by economic, demographic, and social change. Dwindling supplies of water and pasture—the result of desertification in the north—have made it much harder to sustain a nomadic lifestyle, forcing young people to seek wage-paying jobs in urban areas. War in the south has completely disrupted traditional lifestyles. Moreover, social pressures such as the desire to be near medical clinics and regular schools are pulling herders into more permanent settlements.

Sudan also has a growing professional class that includes businessmen and bureaucrats, lawyers and engineers, teachers and students, artists and musicians. Parents have aspirations for their children that go beyond the cattle camp and

Two men converse in the doorway of a traditional Nubian house on the northern Nile.

farm. Schools and universities are producing an urban proletariat, people who are adapting their cultures to new environments.

Civil wars within Sudan and in neighboring states have produced large numbers of displaced people and refugees. More than four million southerners have fled the war in the south, with perhaps three million of them now living in the Khartoum area. The capital, like every other northern city, has been a magnet for people from all regions seeking work. More than a million refugees from civil strife in Chad, Eritrea, and Ethiopia as well as Uganda and the Congo have entered Sudan during the last three decades. While some have returned home, many have stayed and added to the country's ethnic mix, marrying Sudanese as well as their own people. As has happened repeatedly in Sudan, these groups are forging new alliances and identities.

Until recently it was possible to recognize the ethnic affiliation of many Sudanese by the decorative scars on their faces. People throughout Sudan marked their faces by cutting lines and dots on their cheeks and foreheads, often as part of initiation ceremonies, to create simple and elaborate cicatrices. This practice has all but disappeared in towns, and it is very rare today to see teenagers in urban centers with scarifications. The physical markings may be vanishing, but most Sudanese continue to identify themselves with a specific ethnic group or lineage.

Northern Groups

Sudan takes its name from the term given to the area by medieval Muslim geographers: Bilad al-Sudan, "the land of the blacks." Nevertheless, western archaeologists initially saw the ruins found along the Nile in Sudan as an extension of the Egyptian pharaohs' reach. Archaeological evidence collected over the last fifty years, however, shows that Kerma, also called Kush, formed the first great black African kingdom (2500–1500 BCE), and that it both influenced and was influenced by Egyptian culture.

The debate over Kerma's past has important implications both for how foreigners see Sudan and how Sudanese see themselves. David Edwards, in his 2004 study *The Nubian Past,* describes the continuing "Egyptological legacy" as "isolating archaeological research in the Sudan from that of the fledgling African archaeology, especially where it might have shared interests and concerns with other parts of Sudanic Africa." He argues that the focus on Egypt instead of an indigenous civilization has fed modern views that "all too often perceive an 'Arab' north and 'African' south as somehow a natural and timeless condition, rather than a creation of relatively recent history."

Key evidence for Africans in Nubia comes from ancient texts and stone carvings. Soleb, an Egyptian New Kingdom temple on the west bank of the nearby Nile, celebrates Amenhotep III's fourteenth-century-BCE conquest of neighboring peoples. The bound captives shown on his temple columns are clearly black African. Limited mitochondrial DNA studies from the relatively few remains of the later Meroitic period suggest only that black African markers drifted slowly from farther south to the north. The pictorial record, from Egypt and Sudan itself, however, clearly shows "Negroid" facial traits and, where paint remains, black skin.

The medieval Muslim geographers who gave Sudan its name identified four distinct ethnic groups in what is now the northern half of the country: Nubians, Arabs, Beja, and blacks. Today the descendants of these groups all speak Arabic, are Muslim, and claim genealogies linking them to the Prophet Muhammad. Northern Sudanese Arabs generally belong to either the settled people of the main Nile (essentially Arabized Nubians, the Mahas, Danaqla, and the Ja'alyeen group); the once mainly nomadic Juhayna group that originated in southern Arabia; or the Kawahla, a semisedentary group around Khartoum. The Nubians, now heavily intermarried with immigrant Arab tribes who arrived via Egypt from Arabia, trace their lineage to Kush. They occupy the Nile River valley from Dongola to southern Egypt and still speak a mother tongue rooted in the Kushite period. Until recently, Arabic was their second, not first, language and in some cases still is.

The construction of the Aswan Dam in the 1960s and subsequent flooding of the area north and south of the Egyptian border displaced nearly fifty thousand Nubians. Many of them were resettled on the upper Atbara River; others migrated to seek jobs in the cities, where they work in both public and private sectors. There are now more Nubians in Khartoum, Port Sudan, and Kassala than in the Nubian region.

The Ja'alyeen, a collection of sedentary clans who live in the central Nile region, have played a major role in modern Sudanese politics. They claim a common ancestor, Al-Abbas, who was the uncle of the Prophet Muhammad. This use of mythological genealogies exists among all Muslim Sudanese groups, be they from the north, east, or west, complicating arguments about who is Arab and who is African. The Shayqiyya, once centered around the

Fourth Cataract of the Nile, dominated eighteenth-century Nubia. After their failed resistance to the Ottoman invasion in the 1820s, many moved to the Khartoum area in service to the Turco-Egyptians. Today, they play a prominent role in both government and commerce.

The Juhayna, traditionally considered nomadic, are now largely sedentary. They claim descent from the Qahtan and Himyar peoples of southern Arabia and came to Sudan by crossing the Red Sea. They divide into several important subgroups including the Shukriyya and the Baqqara, whose name means "cow herder." The Shukriyya, who have established themselves around the agricultural center of Qadarif, have become largely settled and urbanized, while the Baqqara remain nomadic. The Shukriyya rose to power in the eighteenth century under the leadership of the Abu Sinn family. Their greatest notable, Ahmad Abu Sinn (c. 1790–1870), became a *bey,* or governor, under the Turco-Egyptian authority and ruled Khartoum for ten years.

Thirteen clans belonging to the Kawahla group live in the areas west and south of Khartoum. Historically they have had a mixed pastoralist-sedentary economy, but increasingly they are settling on farms and in the city.

Western Groups

Western Sudan is home to a mix of Juhayna Arab and African peoples. The Kababish, a loose confederation of camel nomads in the western desert, travel great distances in a complex annual migration in search of water and pasture. Although they trace their lineage to the Arabian Peninsula, they have married extensively with north African groups. Traditionally, they lived in tents made of camel skins and cotton cloth. Like most northern nomads, the men wear sheathed daggers on their left arms. The women wear colorful *tobes*—a three-yard length of cotton. The Kababish suffered greatly from the drought in the 1980s, and their camel herds have declined. Many have moved closer to Khartoum in search of work.

The Baqqara, a collection of seven main groups, are cattle nomads whose ancestors probably came from western Nigeria and Chad. Extensive intermarriage with African groups over the centuries has produced a distinctly Afro-Arab culture. The Baqqara live in tents made from sticks, grass, and mats in Kordofan and Darfur, where they occupy an important political space. They often are in competition with their settled African neighbors for resources. Although they are Muslim, they also have witch doctors and healers, part of their African heritage. Some

of their music and dance movements can also be traced to African origins.

Several non-Juhayna peoples live widely dispersed in Kordofan and north Darfur. These nomads are of north Arabian origin, and many of them came into Sudan through Chad and Libya. It is members of these groups, known under the broad term of opprobrium *janjaweed,* who have earned international condemnation for their brutal attacks on elements of the Fur, Massalit, and Zaghawa peoples following an armed insurgency that started in Darfur in 2003.

The Fur based around El Fasher and the Massalit to the south have dynastic pasts and a long history of fierce independence. They supplement their agricultural economy with animal husbandry, and they live in permanent villages. The Massalit, like the Zaghawa, have numerous kinsmen living in neighboring Chad. In contrast to the Fur and the Massalit, the Zaghawa are seminomadic, shuffling back and forth across the Chad border with their cattle, camels, and sheep. In recent years, however, farming has become more important, and they are building more permanent villages.

Some local leaders in Darfur and Kordofan are making valiant efforts to resolve disputes between nomads and pastoralists. The Selamat Messeria, a Baqqara group at Lake Keilak on the southwestern range of the Nuba Mountains, is one nomadic group that is becoming sedentary, engaging in agriculture irrigated by the lake's waters. Young men still take cattle to dry areas during the rainy season to escape the tsetse fly, but 80 percent of the clan stays at their village throughout the year. Not so long ago, only 20 percent would have remained. To establish a broader, settled community among the area's three thousand inhabitants, Bakhiet Fadul al Sid, emir of the Selamat Messeria, has made his own contribution to peace by giving plots of his lands to Dinka and others among the seven ethnic groups that currently live near the lake.

The Nuba

The Nuba Mountains, a thirty-thousand-square-mile scatter of granite outcrops, rise sharply above the plain of southern Kordofan. Over the centuries, dozens of African ethnic groups fleeing slave traders and advancing Arabization have found refuge here, and collectively they are known as the Nuba. Linguists have identified fifty languages and dialects spoken in the Nuba Mountains. The largest of the northern non-Arab groups, the Nuba are farmers who cultivate terraced slopes and fertile valleys.

The Nuba captured the world's imagination in two books (published in the 1970s) by the late, controversial German photographer and filmmaker Leni Riefenstahl. Her photographs caught naked Nuba dancing, fighting bracelet duels, wrestling, and struggling against their harsh living conditions.

The Nuba still celebrate harvests with festivals that include dancing and wrestling matches. During the harvest festival, young men undergo a *passage de vie* that includes strapping a set of bull's horns to their heads to proclaim their manhood. Not so long ago, the women also wrestled, albeit out of sight of the men. Now, they stay on the sidelines, singing and cheering, often wrapped in a traditional northern *tobe,* a mark of the evolution toward clothing over the last thirty years.

Nuba wrestling has become something of a national sport, with numerous teams competing in three provinces. The Khartoum area alone has a dozen teams. Fans from every ethnic background gather on Friday afternoons at an open-air stadium in Haj Yusef to watch their favorite wrestlers. Coaches, referees, and managers operate under a license granted by the minister of sports. In the last few years Baqqara tribesmen have been allowed to

join the Nuba wrestling teams. The organizers, with some seriousness, say they would like to make Nuba wrestling an Olympic sport.

The Takarna and Fellata

Sudan has nearly two million people of West African origin. Most of them immigrated over the last two centuries as pilgrims transiting through Sudan on their way to Mecca to complete that important pillar of Islam, the hajj. About 60 percent came from Nigeria; those from the Hausa ethnic group are called Takarna or Takruri and the rest are known as the Fellata, who may well be the descendants of the Fulani Bedouins of West Africa. The Takarna and the Fellata have heavily settled in several areas of northern and central Sudan, including Kassala and along the White Nile.

Eastern Peoples

Eastern Sudan is home to one of the oldest people in the country, the Beja, and one of the most recent, the Rashaida. The Beja, divided among five main groups and dozens of subgroups and clans, may be the people the ancients knew as the Blemmyes, who overtook Meroe and became protectors of the trade route across the Nubian Desert to the Red Sea. Predominantly camel nomads, the Beja occupy the harsh, arid area of the Red Sea Hills between the borders of Egypt and Eritrea. Some clans roam inland from the coast as far as the junction of the Atbara and Nile rivers. Both the Hadendowa and Beni Amer clans now extend from Port Sudan south to the Gash River delta and the town of Kassala.

Legend has it that the Beja, around the first century CE, became the first camel breeders, giving them control of the desert trade routes extending inland from the Red Sea coast. Like other Arabized Sudanese, they have adopted genealogies linking them to Arab ancestors. Most Beja, however, continue to speak their native language (To-Bedawiye), with Arabic their second tongue.

The Beja put up a spirited but ultimately unsuccessful fight against Turco-Egyptian rule. The Egyptians built the eastern fort-town of Kassala in the early nineteenth century, and it soon developed into the major market it is today. By the early 1880s, Osman Digna, the most famous of the Beja warriors, had united the Beja clans behind the Mahdi (see chapter 1). Imperial Britain dubbed the Beja "fuzzy-wuzzy" in reference to their untamed hair, and Rudyard Kipling, in his verse, commemorated their bravery in battle as "first-class" fighting men. The Haden-dowa, the largest of the Beja clans, also formed the core of defenders against the charge of Britain's 21st Lancers at the battle of Omdurman in 1898. Nearly three-fourths of the Beja, more than four hundred thousand people, died due to war with Britain and drought in the closing years of the nineteenth century.

Beja society, like much of Sudan, is conservative and family oriented. Fathers arrange weddings, and like some central Nile families, cousins often marry. This is due in part to a deep suspicion of outsiders but also to a desire to keep wealth within the extended family. Important values include self-control and bravery, and all men carry long swords. Camels are the backbone of Beja economy and culture, supplying milk, meat, and skins as well as important dowry and trade items.

Port Sudan, built in 1922 to accommodate large ships, is now a Beja stronghold. The Hadendowa, displaced from rural areas by drought and diminishing pasture, have become the city's principal workforce. The Beni Amer to the south straddle the border with Eritrea and are concentrated in the area around Kassala.

The Rashaida emigrated from the Arabian Peninsula only 150 years ago and are among the least integrated of the eastern Sudanese tribes. They live in low-slung tents in the desert from Port Sudan south to Kassala. Alone among Sudanese women, the Rashaida keep their faces covered, revealing only their eyes in public. Rashaida men, like the Beja, carry swords, and they hold sword-dancing competitions to mark any occasion, be it a wedding or an impromptu gathering of foreign visitors. The Rashaida are great traders (some would say smugglers), importing goods from the Arabian Gulf. In addition to herds of camels, the Rashaida now have fleets of Toyota pickups.

The indigenous people in the Ingessana Hills occupy the central area of Sudan's border with Ethiopia. They call themselves Gâmk, the word for "hills," but are known to the outside world as the Ingessana. Like their neighbors the Uduk, they inhabit a buffer area between the north and the south as well as between Sudan and Ethiopia. Both groups live in established settlements and survive on subsistence agriculture. The Rufa'a Arabs from the Blue Nile region have seasonally occupied the plains around the Ingessana Hills since the 1930s. Both farmers and pastoralists are feeling competitive pressures from northern-owned businesses engaged in mechanized agriculture and the livestock industry.

Southern Peoples

Southern Sudan is an ethnic mosaic of myriad groups speaking dozens of languages. Few claim Arab descent, but Arabic is, to a large degree, the lingua franca in urban areas. While some southerners have embraced Islam as a path to and metaphor for modernization, the majority of southerners follow traditional African religions. Many have converted to Christianity, with estimates ranging from 5 to 15 percent. As in the north, southerners are divided between quasi pastoralists and farmers. Ethnographers have identified three main ethnic groupings based on linguistic and cultural similarities. These are the Nilotics of the central area around the Nile, the Nilo-Hamites southeast of the Nile, and the Sudanics of the southwest.

The Nilotics include three of the largest southern peoples, the Dinka, the Nuer, and the Shilluk. These tall, slender people are renowned for their independence, courage, and pride; they have always opposed outside attempts to control them. Although there are some important differences between these groups, all depend on cattle for their basic livelihood and reside near the Nile or its main tributaries in villages of circular *tukuls* made of mud and reeds with grass-thatch roofs. During the dry season, from November to March, they move their cattle nearer to the Nile and its branches. When the rains start in April and these areas become an uninhabitable marsh, the herders seek higher ground. Large cattle byres of prewar days have given over to camps where, at night, cattle are tethered to pegs in the ground, surrounded by dung fires to keep mosquitoes and other biting insects at bay. After the sun rises, young men lead the animals out to graze. Conflicts among these groups historically arose from disputes about cows and pasture.

Aba, village of the Shilluk.
From *Journey to Central Africa*, 1854

Youngsters in a Dinka
cattle camp confrontation.
Photo: Timothy Carney

The Shilluk, unlike the Dinka and the Nuer, have a centralized authority in the figure of the *reth,* their king. For more than three centuries, the Shilluk king has ruled, through a disciplined council of chiefs, from the village of Kodok on the While Nile to an area just south of Malakal, a major administrative and trading center. The king has royal residences in both Kodok and Malakal, in part because travel through the mud and swamp to Kodok during the rainy season is virtually impossible. Shilluk kneel outside the king's court wherever he is to ask favors and plead civil disputes. Shilluk of both sexes wear a toga-like length of cotton cloth knotted at one shoulder. The men once wore cloth dyed in brick dust; today they have adopted a commercially produced pink material. Women wear brightly colored cottons and beaded belts. Older Shilluk are distinguished by a row of beadlike scars across their foreheads.

Malakal sits on the northern fringe of the Sudd, home to the Nuer, that "most amphibious of the Nilotic tribes," as one observer characterized them. They extend to Bentiu on the Bahr al-Ghazal River immediately west of the Sudd. Fierce and independent, the Nuer strongly resisted both Turco-Egyptian slavers and British colonial authorities. Slavers largely left them alone rather than pursue them through the swamp. The British were not able to bring the Nuer under a measure of government control until 1928.

Like other Nilotic cultures, Nuer life has revolved almost completely around cattle. Although the Nuer plant sorghum in small family plots and engage in nominal fishing, a family's wealth is measured in cattle, and society is organized around protecting and acquiring cows, which in turn provide for most material needs. The Nuer diet consists largely of milk and milk products. "The attitude of the Nuer towards, and their relations with, neighboring peoples are influenced by their love of cattle and their desire to acquire them," wrote E. E. Evans-Pritchard in his classic 1940 study of the Nuer. "Nuer tend to define all social processes and relationships in terms of cattle. Their social idiom is a bovine idiom." Although the Nuer worldview has changed little, the civil war has disrupted the traditional rhythm of life, and the development of the oil industry is posing new challenges and opportunities.

Many of the oil fields that have been identified in Sudan lie in the Nuer area. Fields north of Bentiu already produce oil, and with a coalition government, the Sudd will become a focus of international exploration. Development of the oil fields around Bentiu sparked conflict and provoked charges that the Nuer had been forcibly moved. Today, the Nuer are poised to become among the first southerners to benefit directly from the oil industry in the form of schools, hospitals, and other community projects.

The Nuer have always had an intense rivalry with their neighbors and ethnic cousins, the Dinka, for control of pastures. With twenty-five mutually independent groups and countless clans, the Dinka form the largest southern ethnic group. They surround the Nuer, inhabiting 150,000 square miles of savannah grasslands that stretch across much of central southern Sudan. Although the historic Nuer-Dinka competitiveness may be rooted in cows, it today extends into modern national politics. Violent conflict has erupted between the Nuer and Dinka several times throughout the course of the civil war.

The Dinka fought well into the twentieth century against Condominium rule. One of the most celebrated British officers, a scholar as well as a hunter, Major C. H. Stigand, fell to Dinka spears in 1919. Today the Dinka form the core of the southern rebel movement, the Sudan People's Liberation Army (SPLA), and its political wing, the Sudan People's Liberation Movement (SPLM). Like the Nuer, their entire culture is built around cattle herding, and they have an extensive vocabulary to describe the colors, shapes, and sizes of their cows, oxen, and bulls. Dinka men are renowned for the songs they sing to and about their oxen.

The Dinka organize themselves in clans, associations of blood relatives who identify themselves with an animal, bird, or other symbol that members regard as a spiritual ancestor. They keep close track of extensive family trees because it is taboo for members of the same clan in the same region to marry. Marriage, which can take as long as three years to arrange, is an extremely serious business in Dinka society, in part because it is the principal means by which families expand their cattle herds. The kinsmen of the bride receive cattle from the family of the groom.

Dinka boys go through a series of rites of passage to manhood, starting with circumcision around the age of five or six. After their second set of teeth have grown in fully, they undergo a procedure to remove the four lower front teeth. The Dinka believe they are more attractive without these teeth pushing out their lips. Finally, between the ages of sixteen and eighteen, young men are formally initiated as adults. At this time their faces are scarified with seven to ten horizontal cuts across the forehead.

In addition to raising cattle, the Dinka plant tobacco, groundnuts, and sorghum. During the dry season, they also fish in the rivers. They supplement this diet with fruits including tamarind and mango. Women are responsible for all aspects of cooking, from fetching water and grinding sorghum to churning milk into a kind of yogurt. The women make attractive clay pots and wicker baskets,

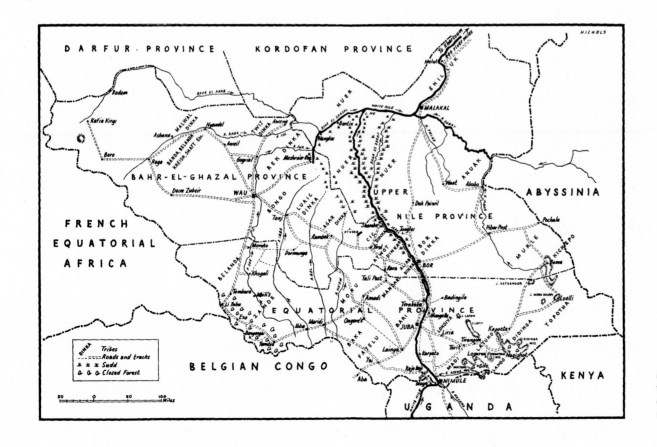

Map of southern Sudan at the time of independence, with ethnic groups listed.
From *The Cry of the Fish Eagle*, 1954

which they carry on their heads, filled with water or produce, or even a baby.

Rumbek is the main commercial center for the Dinka. The town came under SPLA control in mid-1997 and is an SPLM administrative center. Farming activity is increasing the amount of acreage put to the plow, and foreign assistance programs are supporting agricultural cooperative schemes. Rumbek is also a headquarters of international efforts to monitor military agreements between the government and the SPLA/M.

The Nilo-Hamitic group includes numerous peoples who have settled along the southern Nile and in the southeastern quadrant of the country. These include the Bari and the closely related Kuku, Kakwa, and Mandari. The Bari occupy the area around Juba, the main administrative town in the south. Living in close proximity to the Nilotics, the Bari and Mandari have been greatly influenced by them. The Mandari in the area of Terakeka north of Juba, for example, have a cattle camp life that closely mirrors that of the Nuer and the Dinka. The more southerly Kuku and Kakwa are located in the highlands, where farming has been more productive.

The Anuak live to the east on the Ethiopian border, just north of the Murle, who are found to the southeast near the Boma Plateau. The Toposa, neighbors to the south, conduct raids against their ethnic cousins the Jie and the Kachipo, who maintain traditional lifestyles in the Boma Plateau region. The Kachipo, best known internationally for their lip plates, have settled on top of the plateau and extend east to the Ethiopian border. Many Kachipo women, including some in their twenties, still cut their lower lips and insert plates of ivory or wood. The SPLM inveighs against this custom as part of its effort to end what it considers harmful traditional practices. This stand is mirrored in the support of Khartoum authorities for programs to stop the practice of female circumcision in the north.

The Murle, who have immigrated from Ethiopia over the last century, both herd cattle and engage in agriculture over a large region stretching from Pibor in the government zone to the Boma Plateau, effectively splitting them, like many southern groups, between government- and SPLM-controlled areas. Murle elders in Pibor, who for the most part are Presbyterian, were among the first to initiate conversations with their counterparts in the SPLM zone about how to end the war. The Murle, like most southerners, follow the practice of dividing young boys into so-called age sets, or initiation groups. Unlike the Dinka, the Murle only extract two lower teeth in their initiation practices.

Much of the southwest is home to the Azande, the largest subgroup of the Sudanics and descendents of the Ambomo people under the royal house of the Avongara, who began migrating into Sudan from French Equatorial Africa in the sixteenth century. The Azande created their nation by conquering and then imposing their language and political institutions on numerous indigenous ethnic groups. "The cultural amalgamation they accomplished speaks to their superior political organization," wrote anthropologist E.E. Evans-Pritchard. The Azande faced little opposition as they expanded north until they encountered the Arabized people who were thrusting south. The Azande bravely resisted the Turco-Egyptian slave raids.

Azande society traditionally is divided into three main classes: nobles who can trace their ancestry to the royal house; commoners who have Azande lineage; and commoners who are descendants of conquered peoples. Their economy once depended on hunting and agriculture, but today they are primarily farmers. In a bold agricultural experiment in the 1940s, the Azande scheme, they took up cotton growing. The rich soil of the region also produces

Young Azande man playing a large drum at Nzara, c. 1950–59.
University of Durham Sudan Archive

both Arabica and Mocha coffee. Visitors are stunned to see major teak plantations extending from Tambura in the southwest and across western Equatoria to Maridi. Huge mango trees, planted without forethought to shade the roads, make a hazardous course for vehicles when ripe fruit plunges from sixty-five-foot-high trees into windshields.

Spiritual Life

Sudanese adhere to two main monotheistic world religions, Islam and Christianity, and follow traditional African beliefs. About 60 percent of the entire population is Muslim. Most Muslims live in the northern half of the country and most are Sufis, who fall broadly under the Sunni mantle. Sudan has dozens of Sufi orders, called *tariqas,* or devotional paths. Each *tariqa* is led by a *shaykh,* a religious leader who is the spiritual heir of the founder of the order. Sufis seek a close personal relationship with Allah which is sometimes achieved through strenuous group exercises (*dhikr*) that include reciting prayers and repeating the ninety-nine names, or qualities, of Allah.

The Qadiriyya, Sudan's oldest and most widespread Sufi *tariqa,* was established in the sixteenth century. Followers of the Qadiriyya gather at the Hamad el-Nil mosque in Omdurman every Friday at sunset. Dervishes, dressed in brightly colored tunics, dance and swirl themselves into an ecstatic state. At the other end of town, the Sammaniyya, dressed in white *jelabia* and Sam Browne belts, stand in a line before their leader to chant the ninety-nine names of Allah. In a spiritual form of line dancing, they bend, twist, and jump. Nowhere outside of Sudan do Arabs jump. Africans jump, and Sudanese Muslims have incorporated this motion into their religious expression or, as in the east among the Beja and Rashaida, their sword dances.

Other important Sufi orders include the Khatmiyya, Sammaniyya, Tijaniyya, and Idrisi. Ahmad ibn Idris al-Fasi (d. 1837) was a particularly influential Sufi *shaykh* in Saudi Arabia. One of his disciples, Muhammad 'Uthman al-Mirghani (1793–1853), founded the Khatmiyya *tariqa,* which became the backbone of the Democratic Unionist Party. The spiritual leader, or *khalifa,* of the eastern branch of the Khatmiyya lives in Kassala at the *tariqa's* main mosque.

The Muslim reformer Muhammad Ahmad ibn 'Abdallah —known as the Mahdi—owed his religious education to leading Sufi *shaykhs.* The religious movement he

The late Shaykh Hasan Qariballah of the Sammaniyya Sufi sect.
Photo: Timothy Carney

founded in the 1880s blended elements of Sufi tradition with a political agenda. The descendants of his followers are generally members of the modern Umma political party and are called Ansaris, just as the Mahdi's followers were.

Modern Islamist organizations exist alongside the traditional and, like the Khatmiyya and the Ansar, play an important role in Sudanese politics. The present government in Khartoum is led by members of the National Congress Party, an organization that evolved from the National Islamic Front, which in turn grew out of the Sudanese branch of Egypt's Muslim Brotherhood.

Sudan has long been noted for its *faki,* pious men who possess *baraka,* or holiness, and perform *karamat,* or miracles. These men are often teachers and headmasters at *khalwas,* religious schools for boys. These schools, where boys memorize the Qur'an and its teachings, have played an important historical role in the development and spread of Islam in Sudan and continue to be a significant cultural and religious force.

Christians, including Copts, Roman Catholics, Protestants, and evangelicals, are all present in Sudan. The north still has a substantial Coptic population. Originally immigrants from Egypt and elsewhere in the Middle East, Coptic Christians run important businesses, often work in public service, and contribute to the rich cultural tapestry of the country. The archbishop of the Coptic Church presides over services at the main cathedral in Khartoum, and there are two other large Coptic churches in the capital area.

Writing boards for Islamic studies rest against a shelter at the Abu Shouk camp for internally displaced persons, North Darfur. Millet grows in the foreground.
Photo: Timothy Carney

The Roman Catholic Church has been active in Sudan since 1647, when the first Franciscan missionaries arrived in Suakin. These missionaries and their successors persevered through great hardship to establish a Catholic presence throughout the country. Sudan has given the church two saints—Bishop Daniel Comboni (canonized 2003) and Sister Josephine Bakhita (canonized 2000)—and one cardinal, installed in 2003 when the pope elevated the archbishop of Khartoum, Gabriel Zubeir Wako, to the position.

No other modern Christian has had as great an impact on Sudan as Daniel Comboni (d. 1881). Born in Italy in 1831, he arrived in Sudan as a young missionary in 1857. He founded the Comboni Missionaries, established the first church school in the country, and became bishop of Khartoum in 1877. The Combonis have set up churches, elementary and secondary schools, and health clinics in major towns throughout the north and south. The cathedral in El Obeid is considered one of the most beautiful buildings in Sudan, and the church in Malakal draws a full house of worshipers every Sunday. A Comboni-run theological seminary in the capital trains young men from around the country to become priests.

At the turn of the twentieth century, Condominium authorities set up arbitrary zones of religious influence in Sudan. They declared everything north of the tenth parallel to be Islamic and divided the south into three zones, given respectively to the British Missionary Societies, the Austrian Catholic Missionaries, and the American Mission. American Presbyterians set up a station at Doleib Hills,

in the south. Although most of the old missionary outposts have fallen into disrepair, they continue to serve local communities. In many cases, such as at Loli, a village on the White Nile north of Malakal, a dilapidated church does double duty as a school, with the headmaster, who is also a priest, conducting religious services on Sunday.

Every major town in Sudan has at least one Roman Catholic and one Protestant church. The Anglicans are particularly focused on building schools and health clinics. Many have established links with churches in the United States and Europe whose congregations ship clothes, books, and medical supplies to Sudan and also provide funds for special projects. Several evangelical Christian groups, such as Reverend Franklin Graham's Samaritan's Purse, are active in the north and south and are providing aid in Darfur.

The majority of southern Sudanese continue to observe traditional religions. With variations, they believe that a great and very remote "sky god" created and exercises power over humanity. A number of spirits and messengers serve as intermediaries in an indeterminate realm between this god and the people. It is through chiefs, prophets, diviners, magicians, and other ritual experts that ordinary men and women communicate with the spirits. Every group has its shrines and sacred places where people make sacrificial offerings to mark important occasions as well as to seek the god's help.

The Dinka, for example, believe in a monotheistic supreme being, Nhialic, and say "God is one." However, as the noted Dinka scholar, Francis Deng has observed, the Dinka religion is not focused on the afterlife. The Dinka rely on a pantheon of divinities and ancestor spirits to ensure prosperity in this world and the perpetuation of their people through living descendants.

Chiefs, prophets, and magicians play important roles as intermediaries with the god throughout the south. For the Nuer, a prophet is a man who has been possessed by one of the sky spirits, whom they see as the sons of the sky god. One class of these prophets is called *cok kwoth,* literally "ants of god." The Dinka believe that a prophet is some-one who has been possessed or "caught by the spirit."

Animal sacrifice to the spirits, followed by feasting and dancing, marks every important stage of life among the southern ethnic groups. Sheep, goats, and cows are sacrificed to carry messages to the various spirits who will mediate with the god on behalf of the people. Communal sacrifices ensure good rains and bountiful harvests. Sacrifices mark births, initiation ceremonies, marriages, and deaths. The importance of the occasion and the wealth of the individual determine both the kind of animal and number sacrificed. A poor family may offer only a sheep or a goat on the birth or death of a family member. A wealthier family will sacrifice a bull and invite the extended kinship group to the feast.

Rites of Passage

Sudanese, like people everywhere, mark life's most important events from birth to death with rituals, ceremonies, and festivals. The similarities among the different ethnic groups are often as striking as the differences. Sudanese from all regions and religions celebrate almost every occasion with food, music, and dance. Musicians beat basic rhythms on ceremonial drums of every imaginable size and shape. Flutes, chordophones, and animal-horn instruments add depth to the music. James Dempsey, a Catholic missionary who lived with the Shilluk in the 1940s, observed, "The Shilluk is fonder of dancing, we may suppose, than of anything else in the world." He could just as easily have been describing any other Sudanese people. From the Beja and Rashaida to the Nuba and the Dinka, all Sudanese literally leap at the chance to dance.

Births

The birth of a child, especially the firstborn, is always an important occasion. The Azande wait a week, or until the newborn's umbilical cord sloughs off, before holding a naming ceremony. The whole family gathers outside the natal hut. A female relative carries the baby from the hut to an arch built of wild sugar cane for the occasion. There, the child is perfumed in the smoke from a small fire of leaves and grasses selected to impart protections and virtues. After the smoking, the baby is laid in a furrow in the earth to ensure that he or she remains anchored to the homeland, a source of future strength. The baby is returned to the arch, where a young girl carrying a tray of food leaps over the infant and the smoldering fire. She takes the food to the compound gate at the roadside, offering it to passersby and children. The diners eat a few bites and, without washing their hands, greet the mother, smearing their fingers on her breasts and on the baby. The child thus has two opportunities to be infused with the supreme virtue of generosity, through its own skin and from its mother's milk. Only then does the baby receive its name. Christians follow the same ritual, with a pastor baptizing the child later in the day.

People in the far north, Darfur, and Kordofan have similar customs for naming newborns. In some cultures, the family will sacrifice an animal to mark a birth, particularly of a firstborn child. Feasting is often followed by dancing.

Circumcision and Initiation

Sudanese have an array of circumcision and initiation rites both for children and young adults. In the Muslim north, all young boys are circumcised. Once the province of religious leaders, most circumcisions in urban areas are now done by doctors. In Khartoum, families take young boys, dressed in crisp white *jelabia* and draped with beads, to the clinics. The boys are compensated for the pain with presents and a party. This custom has spread south. A hundred years ago the Azande did not circumcise boys. Today, they have elaborate ceremonies complete with special adornments, dances, and songs to mark circumcisions. Some Dinka clans have also begun circumcising their boys.

Throughout much of northern Sudan, young girls since pharaonic times have been circumcised. This practice, known as female genital mutilation in the West, is officially opposed by the government and by many Islamic religious leaders. The Qur'an explicitly prohibits body mutilations, but the practice, designed in part to keep girls "pure," is deeply embedded in the Nilotic cultures from Egypt (including the Copts) to Kenya. The Mahdi himself forbade, with limited success, his followers from circumcising their girls. Several Sudanese institutions, including the Ministry of Health and universities, are working with international organizations such as UNICEF to end the practice. One of the country's oldest voluntary organizations—the Sudanese National Association for the Eradication of Harmful Practices—was established to combat female circumcision. Ahfad, the oldest indigenously founded women's university in Africa, has also been at the forefront of the campaign against female circumcision.

In the south, young men, usually between fourteen and sixteen years old, are initiated into manhood through a series of ordeals that used to include scarification of the forehead and/or the removal of teeth. Today teenage boys go out to initiation schools in the bush after the rainy season ends, at the end of October or early November, to fend for themselves for a month. Families welcome initiates back into villages with celebratory feasts and dancing. Each boy receives an ox and a spear, signifying that he has become a warrior.

Initiations play a key role in the organization of society because they determine the age-set to which a man belongs. Elders assign young men to an initiation group and decide when to close the ranks of one group and open another. By going through an initiation period with his contemporaries, a man becomes a member of an age-set, a prerequisite for becoming a leader. Many urbanized young men no longer go through initiation rites, some by choice and others by circumstance. The consequence is that they are no longer fully integrated into traditional structures.

Marriage

Marriage in Sudan is the culmination of a series of choreographed events. In the north, among the Arabs, the fathers of the bride and groom gather with male relatives and friends to negotiate and sign a marriage contract. The young man and woman are prepared for marriage in separate celebrations. The groom has an evening with his male relatives and friends, who apply henna to the soles of his feet and the palms of his hands. Depending on the wealth of the families, there may be several days of parties with music, dancing, and feasting. Families will often go into debt to pay for a wedding.

The bride, who also has her hands and feet decorated with henna, has a women's night attended by female friends but also including her immediate male relatives and the groom. Traditionally, the bride wears red, but increasingly, central Sudanese women are wearing Western-style bridal gowns. In the old days, the bride, wearing nothing but a skirt of leather strips called a *rahat,* would dance for her future husband and the women in attendance. Today the women generally wear tight, sequined dresses with plunging necklines and short skirts. It is the first and last time they appear in public this way.

No prenuptial agreement in the West is more fiercely negotiated than the dowry for a southern bride. Weddings are the principal way in which the Nilotic cattle peoples increase their herds, and the dickering between the families of the groom and the bride can take weeks, months, and even years. It is rarely a simple exchange between two fathers. Rather, the extended families of the groom will be asked to contribute cows to the bride's father, who in turn will have to distribute the dowry among his brothers and cousins.

Girls in the north commonly wore the leather thong *rahat* until marriage.
From *Everyday Sudan Life,* 1937

In Rumbek, complicated negotiations we witnessed did not finish until the day of the wedding. The two families sat opposite each other, aided in their discussions by a vocal and clever intermediary, haggling over the delivery schedule of the cattle, while the bride, dressed in white, waited in a nearby hut. When the deal was finally struck, the frazzled bride was allowed to emerge. Her palms and the soles of her feet had been stained with henna, a cultural borrowing from the north.

Death

Funerals, as everywhere in the world, are religious and cultural occasions that involve extended family and a network of friends. Muslims must be buried within twenty-four hours of death, as is the case with some traditional Nilotics. Close relatives gather for the ritual washing of the body and then accompany it to the cemetery for burial and the final journey. The family of the deceased returns home to receive guests paying condolences. This paying of condolences is a serious social obligation and can go on for several days.

Among southerners, funerals may last several days. During a typical Shilluk funeral, for example, people mourn for three days and then bury the body on the fourth. On that day, the women of the family will make huge vats of sorghum beer, and the men will sacrifice a sheep or a bull. The number of animals sacrificed is a reflection of the age and importance of the deceased and the wealth of his or her family. The sacrificed animal will help carry the deceased to heaven. A crowd will gather at the family compound to drink while the women prepare the food. Mourners start dancing after the feast. "If no funeral rites are made," a Shilluk elder explained, "there is no chance to get to God." This sentiment resonates throughout Sudan.

Arab or African?

Foreigners often ask individual Sudanese whether they are Arab or African. It is a question the Sudanese themselves ponder, overwhelmed at times by the vastness of their geography and the magnitude of their diversity. But it may not be the right question. Just as no northern Sudanese would consider himself a Saudi or Kuwaiti, no southerner would think of himself as a Kenyan or Congolese. More and more northerners refer to themselves as Afro-Arab, which while an accurate description, does not necessarily explain what it means to be Sudanese.

All these people live in the vast Nile River basin, lured and pushed over the millennia from the north, south, east, and west. In this huge mixing bowl they have adapted to different geographic conditions; adopted various religious, cultural, and ethnic identities; and, to varying degrees, warred with each other for as long as history has been recorded. In this crucible, certain indefinable qualities have nevertheless emerged that transcend race, religion, and ethnicity. Despite all the fighting, Sudanese from one end of the Nile to the other have the well-earned reputation of being among the most hospitable and generous people on earth. They possess a certain smile and warmth in the eyes and, in recent years, a growing recognition of belonging to something larger than just one ethnic group. It will be up to the country's political, cultural, and spiritual leaders to ensure that their definition of the nation has enough room for all of them to be counted as Sudanese.

A turban and long smock, or *jelabia*, both in white, constitute the traditional dress of northern men.

Above, Friday prayers at the Ansar mosque in Omdurman.

Hostesses at a bar in Yambio
prepare themselves for the
evening.

Daybreak at Kegel al-Khail, opposite, in the western Nuba Mountains.

A group of travelers finish lunch at a roadside restaurant between Omdurman and Dongola.

A young Murle woman wears
a bead headset in the colors
of the age set to which her man
belongs.

Overleaf:
A Mandari wrestler at a cattle
camp near Terekeka, in the
southern state of Bahr al-Jabal.

Three-wheel auto rickshaws from
India serve as taxis in Khartoum
and Omdurman.

A young Jie woman at the fence
of her small compound, at the
foot of the Boma Plateau.

A Rashaida woman at an encampment of this nomadic tribe near Port Sudan.

A Nubian man setting off from his village near the northern border with Egypt.

Overleaf:
A Rashaida sword dance, during which the men, one at a time, display their prowess as others clap and chant *"Bab Al-Haida"*— Gate of Paradise.

A young man of the Beni Amer
clan of the Beja people in the
market at Kassala.

Beja men often carry nineteenth-century swords, the handles fitted locally to imported steel blades. Authorities maintain that only rarely do those carrying weapons use them.

A minister of the Shilluk kingdom, seated outside the king's residence in Malakal, wears the bright pink that has become the traditional tribal dress.

The dry-season residence of the Shilluk king at Kodok, downriver from Malakal. The tiered apex to the conical thatch roof, above, signifies its royal status.

Shilluk women dancing.

Young Dinka boy, Rumbek.

Dinka women on the way
to market near Rumbek.

A Dinka tobacco seller at
Rumbek market.

Young Dinka woman near
Rumbek.

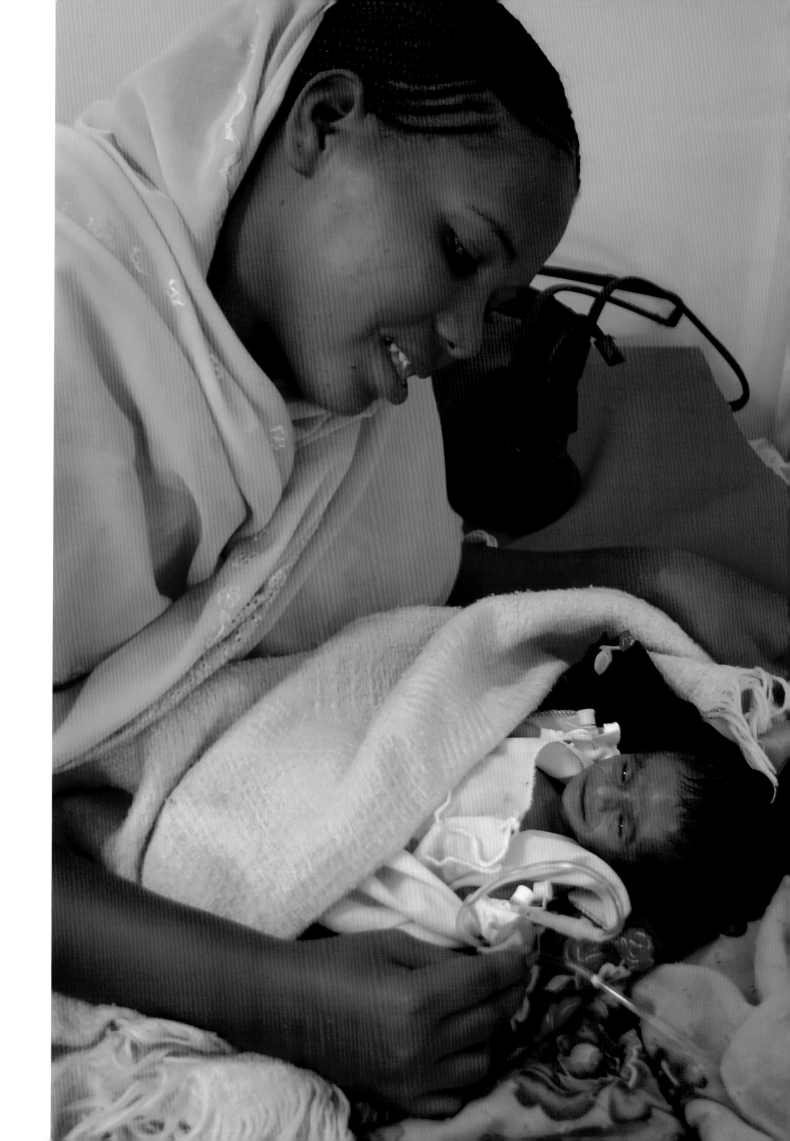

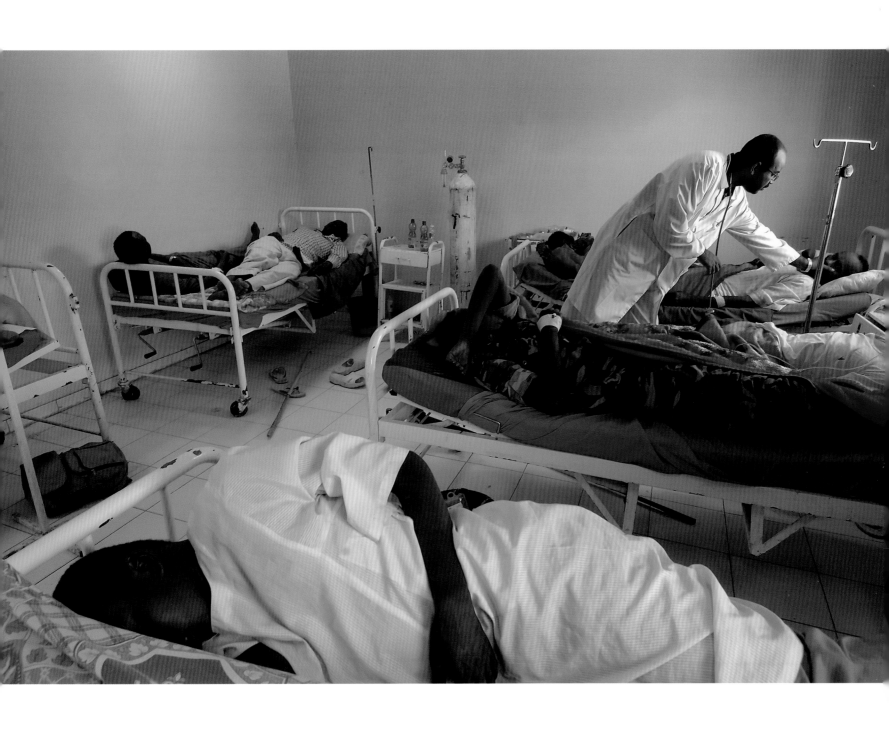

A young Nuer mother, opposite,
tends her child, who has developed marasmus, a serious form
of malnutrition that causes
emaciation.

The newly built oil-company
clinic near the Heglig fields
attracts so many patients from
the surrounding region that
these Nuer malaria sufferers
must sleep two to a bed.

Mandari boys wash head and
hands in fresh cattle urine, later
applying ash from a cow-dung
fire to keep insects away.
Repeated washing has an
admired bleaching effect on
the hair.

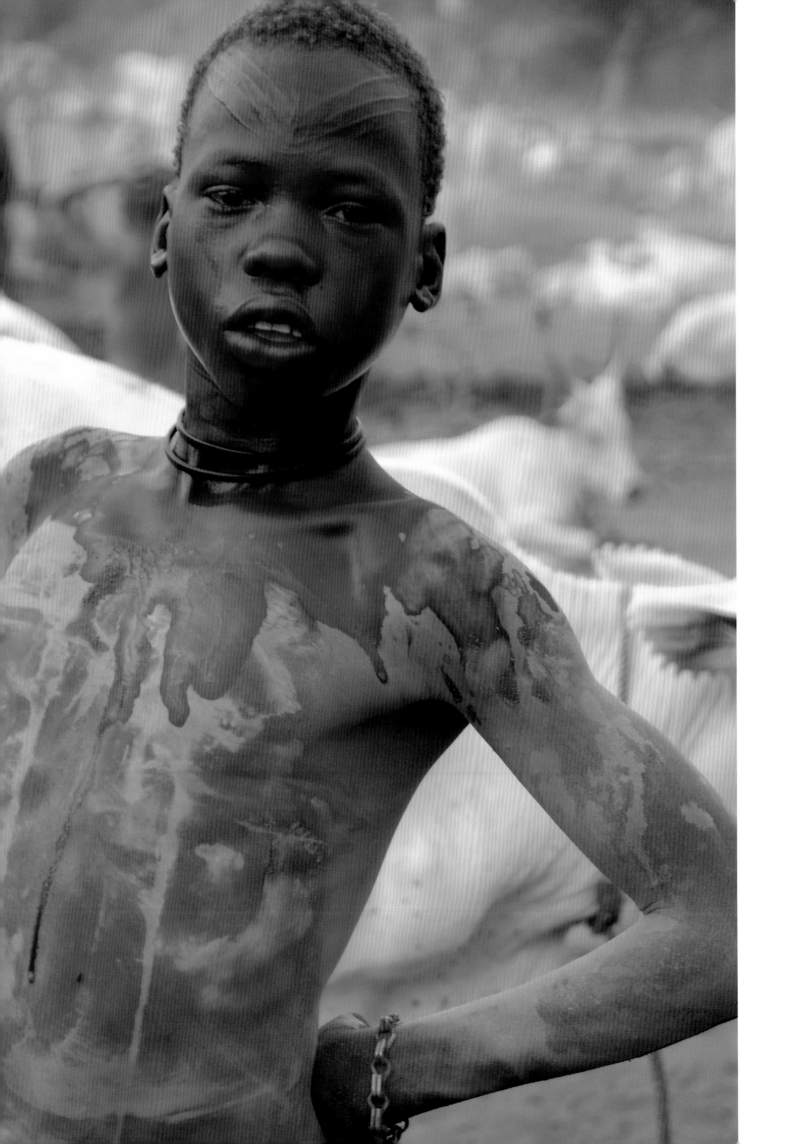

A Mandari boy leads a calf to its tethering post.

Mandari wrestling matches are carefully regulated to ensure tempers do not get out of hand. A regular event between cattle camps, the matches test the strength and combat skills of young men.

Music from horns and drums
accompanies bouts. They rarely
last longer than a minute and are
won when one of the combatants
throws or wrestles his opponent
to the ground.

Opposite, a young woman from Darfur at a displaced persons camp.

Above, the market at El Fasher, capital of North Darfur.

A woman arranges piles of okra for sale at El Fasher market.

Kegel al-Khail village in the
western Nuba Mountains wakes
up on harvest festival day.

Men from the village, wearing grass skirts and headdresses fashioned from cattle horns, perform the Kambala dance, a Nuba tradition that marks the induction of boys into manhood.

Nuba wrestling in Khartoum, a public sport for more than thirty years, has outgrown its origins in the Nuba Mountains to attract spectators from all ethnic groups. Excitement runs high as the afternoon draws on, with stewards hard-pressed to keep order.

Overleaf:
A young Kachipo woman on the Boma Plateau, wearing a plastic ear plug.

Murle girls at Iiti village near the foot of the Boma Plateau.

Above left, a Jie girl from
Nawiaporo village at the
community well, a social
gathering place as much
as a source of water.

Above right, another young
Jie girl cleans gourd containers
used for sorghum mash.

Firearms stand ready for defense
against raiding neighbors. A
Toposa group was said to have
attacked this Jie village the
previous night, with some killed
or wounded.

Overleaf:
Members of a Murle age-set get
together for songs, accompanied
by gourd rattles. The men wear
head rings made from the white
fur of colobus monkeys.

A Jie teenager wears ear, nose, and lip rings in addition to bead necklaces and head and arm bands.

Repairing a reed fence around one of the tightly packed dwellings in the village.

Sorghum mash, probably on its way to becoming the thick, grain beer called *marissa*.

Two Jie boys help each other with their hair decoration.

Two men enjoy a freewheeling
discussion after drinking beer.

Some five to seven thousand
people live in the reed and
thatch community of Nawiaporo
village. Cattle pens are clustered
close to the settlement to afford
the livestock better protection
against raids.

Name day for an Azande child begins six days after birth or when the umbilical cord sloughs off. The child is perfumed in the smoke of medicinal fruits and grasses outside the hut where he or she was born. Following this, a girl carrying a tray of cooked maize (above) leaps over the baby. After family and passersby eat a bit of the maize, they smear the baby's body and the mother's breasts with it, to infuse a spirit of generosity both directly and through the milk.

The child is laid briefly in a furrow to connect it to the land on which it will grow up. For this Christian family, the actual naming will take place in a separate gathering later in the day.

A father in Omdurman comforts his young son who has just undergone circumcision at a doctor's surgery. The white smock and red headband are the traditional dress for this vital rite of passage for any Muslim male.

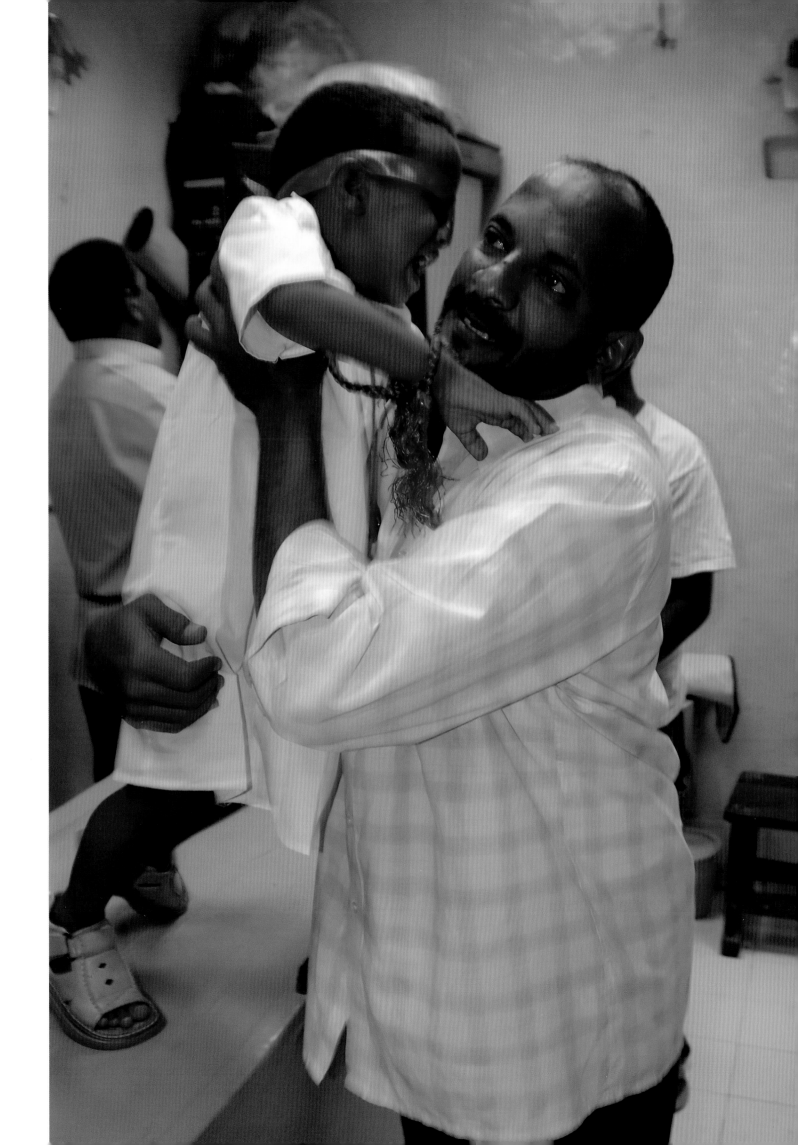

The women's night at a Khartoum
wedding, as friends gather and
an older woman prepares to
anoint the bride with oil.

A bride enters her wedding reception in Omdurman.

Waiters serve dinner to wedding guests.

Hot and tired, the bride waits
inside the family *tukul* as dowry
negotiations between the two
families drag on for hours.

The marriage agreement
finally settled at the close of
day, the couple are escorted
by friends and family to the
reception nearby.

Friday prayer at the Ansar
mosque in Omdurman.

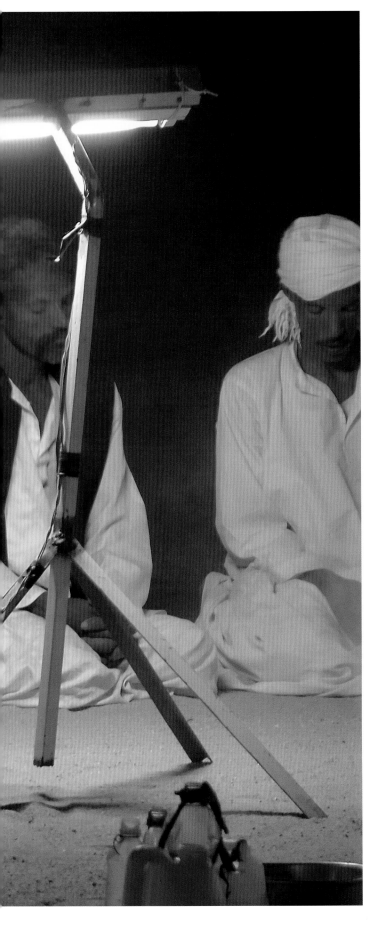

Sufi poetry readings at the Khatmiyya mosque in Kassala.

A merchant in Omdurman *suq* on a Friday reads the Qur'an as he waits for customers.

Overleaf:
A Friday *dhikr* of the Sammaniyya Sufi sect, led by the late Shaykh Hasan Qariballah in Omdurman. *Dhikr* (literally "remembrance") is a Sufi practice in which the names of God or Qu'ranic phrases are chanted as a means of prayer and meditation, here accompanied by jumping in unison.

Overleaf:
Each Sufi sect, or *tariqa,* has its own version of *dhikr.* The Sammaniyya don Sam Browne belts and jump (left), while at the mosque of Hamad el-Nil (right) a Qadiriyya adherent whirls in prayer.

An Anglican pastor reads from the Bible during a naming ceremony for a newborn child in Maridi.

The start of the Roman Catholic
Sunday service in Malakal.

The Roman Catholic cathedral
in El Obeid, completed in 1961
by the Comboni order. It replaced
the church destroyed by the
Mahdi's forces in 1884.

A processional through the
Coptic cathedral in Khartoum
at Christmas.

Opposite, a censer, known to Copts as a *shoriya*, is carried in procession through the cathedral.

The Coptic archbishop, left, enters the cathedral to celebrate Christmas midnight mass.

As the mass proceeds, above, one young member of the congregation finds the hour too late.

An Azande magician and healer,
a leper, shows items that enable
his powers. He is teaching his
son, at left, to follow his calling.

Examination time at the Kenana
Sugar Company school for the
children of employees.

Recitation from the Qur'an at a
government primary school in
Wad Abu Salih.

The classroom at Loli village on
the White Nile, run by a Roman
Catholic priest at a former
missionary outpost.

A young student at Rumbek's
school under the mango tree.

Overleaf:
The end of the day's classes at
Um Dalam village, Kordofan.

305

Khartoum University, founded as Gordon Memorial College by the British, developed a formidable reputation throughout the Middle East and North Africa. Many of its graduates hold senior positions in government and business throughout the Arabian Peninsula states.

Ahfad University for women in Omdurman now teaches 4,600 women from all over the country. Blue jeans and the Muslim *jilbab* headscarf mix easily and on equal terms.

A class in cardiopulmonary resuscitation at the School of Medicine. Ahfad, founded as a university in 1966, grew from a primary school created for the daughters of Babiker Badri, a leading figure in Sudanese education.

A violinist at Ahfad University.

Young Mandari men and women in a jumping dance, accompanied by drums and songs.

Among a group of Shilluk dancers, outside the king's Malakal residence, one woman improvises a neon tube as a baton.

Overleaf:
Rings of monkey fur twirl and fly on the heads of Murle musicians performing in a village in eastern Equatoria.

A Mandari man carries a wind instrument fashioned from a cattle horn that has been extended with plastic tubing to deepen its strong bass.

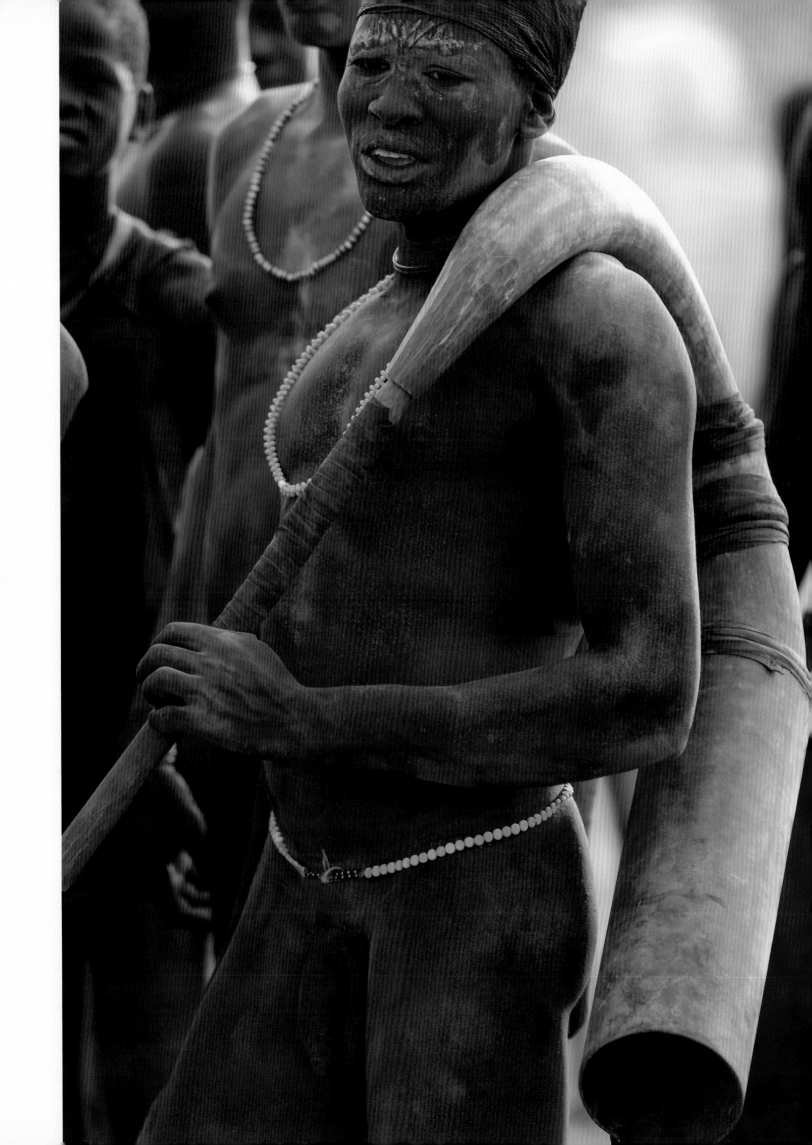

Leading painter Rashid Diab finds inspiration in the rich colors of Sudan, in particular those of women wearing the *tobe*, the traditional garment.

Dressed in a rainbow-hued *tobe*,
a woman in a northern Nubian
village prepares tea for guests.

The head of a Dorcas gazelle, opposite, decorates the painted wooden gate of a house in the Red Sea Hills.

A compound in Nubia with freshly repainted walls. The designs and colors vary from village to village, according to the fashion of the year and the creativity of the householder.

By tradition, only married women apply henna decoration—here on the hands of a bride in Khartoum.

The thick henna paste, prepared from the Lawsonia shrub, is applied through a small hole at the end of a twist of plastic. Dried and fixed in smoke from a charcoal brazier, the pattern can last a few weeks if not washed vigorously.

Overleaf:
A young Mandari woman near Juba, with decorative chevron scars.

Camel breeder in Omdurman.

PHOTOGRAPHER'S NOTE

An opportunity such as this—a large and rich subject that for some reason is untouched—comes only rarely to photographers. The reason here was the ugly one of civil war, a conflict that had persisted for longer than in any other African nation, but for which there was the hope of an end. No book of photo-reportage had been published about any part of Sudan for more than thirty years, and never had there been an attempt to make a book on the full country. The last time that I had had a similar opportunity was in Cambodia, where for much the same reasons the temples of Angkor had been virtually inaccessible for two decades from the beginning of the 1970s. In both instances, for me as a photographer the projects depended utterly on access. The descent of Sudan since independence into civil conflict, so well documented in the opening essay, gradually closed it off to the kind of exploration that we have come to take for granted in reportage photography. Coincidentally, this period, in the last half of the twentieth century, was that of the magazine photo-essay, a form that at its best combined art and journalism and which, sadly, has declined in the face of television reportage. Books are now the vehicle for this kind of photography, and a book was what we planned to do.

But I knew nothing about Sudan and, indeed, very little about Africa. I met Tim Carney and Vicki Butler long ago in Thailand, at the beginning of my obsession with Southeast Asia, when Vicki was the Time-Life stringer and had been deputed to look after me on a long assignment photographing one of the hill-tribes. Tim, over the course of his diplomatic career, had moved between Southeast Asia and Africa, and it was only in April 2002 that Sudan entered my frame of vision. It was in Washington, where first Vicki, then Tim, suggested the idea. I hardly knew what to think, other than that it was a project I could not pass up.

Whatever vague ideas I might have had about how Sudan might be to work in, the reality was more attractive than I had imagined. Obviously, Tim and Vicki wanted me at some level to feel the affection and empathy which they clearly had for the country. Affection is not, by the way, a prerequisite for reportage photography, but it certainly makes it easier to stay committed over the long term. If they ever did worry about that (I didn't ask), it was unnecessary. On our first trip I became entranced. Every nation has its complex and unique character—that's partly how nations come to be—but Sudan was, and is, something special. This is a highly partisan view, impossible to substantiate, but at root, making a book like this draws ultimately on subjectivity. The Sudanese are, as I hope the photographs here convey, highly individual people, very far from homogenous but sharing a Sudanese context that, as Tim and Vicki point out, is elusive to describe. The ethnic diversity was very easy on the camera, and while the landscape was vast, and occasionally had spectacle, it was always the people who held the center of my attention.

Over a period of two and a half years, we spent twenty weeks shooting, in conditions I can describe best as varied. Early on, I had taken the decision to shoot digitally, and the book is the better for it. Digital cameras can operate in lighting conditions that would be impractical for color film, and there are many images here to which I owe that decision.

Michael Freeman

ACKNOWLEDGMENTS

A large cross section of Sudanese, representing every region, religion, and political perspective in the country, made this book possible. They opened their homes and invited us to weddings, name-day celebrations, circumcisions, harvest festivals, and funerals. They took us to into their schools and businesses. They allowed us to photograph their mosques and churches as well as their hospitals and graveyards. With patience and hospitality, Sudanese everywhere answered endless questions and tried to help us understand a very complicated country.

This book, from its inception, had the support of the political leadership in both the north and the south. We are especially grateful to Vice-President 'Ali Osman Taha and Dr. Samson Kwaje, Secretary for Information and Culture and spokesman of the Sudan People's Liberation Movement Army. They both gave unreserved support to this project long before there was a comprehensive peace agreement. They ensured that we had access to the entire country and never once tried to influence what pictures would or would not be taken.

A number of officials in both the north and the south have become friends, and they helped us in countless ways. In Khartoum, Minister of Cabinet Affairs Yahia Hussein Babiker; Ambassador Omer Bireedo and his wife, Khaltoum Barakat; and our companion Major Badr el-Din Hassan 'Abd el-Hakom and his family deserve special mention for everything from arranging travel permits to hosting us for family dinners. In the south, Obed Kundu was an invaluable cultural bridge who built local enthusiasm for the pictures we sought.

Minister of Energy Awad Ijaz and his capable press officer Muhammad Ahmed Siddiq were very supportive. The governors of Kassala, North Darfur State, South Darfur State, Kordofan, the Northern State, and Upper Nile lodged us in their guest houses and extended many courtesies. Similarly, the SPLM County Secretary for Yambio, Mary Biba, and the County Secretary for Maridi, Samuel Bati, together with his colleague James Benson Balubé, Sudan Relief and Rehabilitation Secretary for the area, could not have been more helpful. Dut Maker Ater Dut introduced us to Rumbek. Menalem Ngatul, SPLM Civil Administrator for Jongolei on the Boma Plateau, took us to areas where the local people had never seen a camera. Commander Konyi Dede, as Sudan Relief and Rehabilitation Commission Secretary, made a perceptive host for the entire area of the Boma Plateau.

We could not have taken any of these pictures without the contributions from our sponsors (see page 329). Some provided much more than financial support. Pieter and Rose Stapel of the Hilton Khartoum, our very first sponsors, helped start the project by giving us room and board on our first photographic trip. They continued to host us at reduced rates on every trip we made to the north. We owe the entire Hilton Khartoum staff for a thousand kindnesses as we do their colleagues at the Hilton Port Sudan and the Hilton Nairobi under Olivier Vetter. We have never been treated better in any hotel anywhere in the world. We deeply thank Osama Daoud Abdel Latif of the DAL Group and his wife, Samia, for their incredible hospitality and unfailing support.

El-Tahir Ali el-Tahir of Nasr Construction Company was among the first to share our vision of this book, and no one did more to make it a reality. He became a sponsor, and he took precious time to take us to places rarely visited by foreigners. His representative in Port Sudan, El Tahir Abdel Gader, guided us and then arranged a trip overland from Port Sudan to Kassala, and Qadarif. El Tahir's relatives in Kassala, including the ninety-year-old Mohamed Mahasos and his son, Osman Mahasos, treated us to a traditional lunch at their farm. El Tahir introduced us to Yousif Ahmed Yousif of Higleig Petroleum Services, who in turn embraced the book and made sure that we got pictures not only of the important oil fields but also his hometown near Dinder. We spent a memorable Christmas in Dinder National Park with El Tahir and Yousif, and we thank them. Muhammad Heiba was the first sponsor to give us financial support. He believed in this book from the beginning, and we only hope that the pictures justify his faith in us.

Muhammad O. Suleiman took time off from running his company, Development Technology and Services International, to guide us through eastern Kordofan and the Nuba Mountains. His family and friends in El Obeid, Ali Mahdi and Hisham Omer Hashim Amin, offered regional insights as well as excellent meals. Father Michael Gonzi informed us about the Combonis in El Obeid. Ibrahim Limona, who tends gum arabic trees, gave us much of his time. Mohamed Daoud Muhammad Samel of Dal village and his family provided lodging and refreshments in the Northern State. The late Shaykh Hasan Qariballah welcomed us yet again to the Sammaniyya Friday Dhikr and offered his hospitality afterward. Anis Haggar and his staff, particularly Hanan Abbas, were among our early supporters and remain in our affection. The Indian oil company ONGC Nile Ganga B.V. provided a car and a driver in Khartoum, and D. S. Sangwan and Suresh Batra afforded welcome hospitality. Kenana Sugar Company's Osman Abdalla El Nazir was an early host, and his information officer Hamoeda Muhammad Abdallah gave us assistance beyond the call of duty. Kevin Murphy's loan of cell phones aided communication. The Acropole Hotel's George Pagoulatos offered his charming personality and local knowledge. We also thank those who rescued us from various soft sands, including Shaykh Hasan Muhammad Basher and Shaykh Al-Guriad Mujadid al-Obeid Hamid, both from Khawaldia, and Abdo Gab Bashare and Ghalib Haj Salih in Nubia.

Several nongovernmental organizations lent a helping hand. Ruth Obwayo in Nairobi's CARE office organized our first trip into the south. The Catholic Relief Service staff shared food, accommodations, and insight in the south. Veterinaires sans Frontieres gave us use of a vehicle in the Boma area. Oxfam, Samaritan's Purse, and the International Rescue Committee gave us assistance in Darfur. Monica Ayen Magwat, beneficiary of Catholic Relief Service's Panda project in Rumbek, showed us how development assistance can make a difference. We are particularly grateful to Dr. Omer Suleiman of Development Action Now, whose work in the Nuba Mountains demonstrates the possibilities of fostering peace among various ethnic groups through economic development that can be shared by all. Global 2000's Raymond Stewart and the Ministry of Health's Makoy Samuel Yibi in Juba taught us that, even under difficult circumstances, focused health programs can significantly reduce debilitating diseases. In Malakal, Global 2000's Peter Jaliat gave us welcome assistance. Tom Crick of the Carter Center helped secure an important foreword for the book.

Many others in Sudan shared insights and hospitality. They include Kanza and Hisham Aboulela; Marguerite D'Amelio; Dr. Amna Badri and Dr. Gasim Badri; former Prime Minister Al Sadiq al-Mahdi and his wife, Sara; Mahmoud Saleh and his family; Johnny and Kohar Bodourian; Professor Charles Bonnet; the American Embassy's Elizabeth Colton, Jacquie Poole, Michelle Stefanick, Bob Whitehead, and many old colleagues among the Sudanese staff; British Ambassador William Patey and his wife, Vanessa; Mr. and Mrs. Nadim Ghantous; Miles Donnelly; Tigani El Karib; the late Professor Francis Geus and his wife, Carla; Rushdi Hamid; Professor Friedrich W. Hinkel; Charles and Norma Kfouri; Jonathan Knight; George Limnios and his family; Pierre Loisy; Carol and Eoin Mekie; Dr. Mahir M. Saad and his wife, Dr. Nadia El Dawi; Deborah Scroggins; and Ronnie and Charlie Shaoul.

Indispensable in travel as well as friendship were Sudan's Charge d'Affaires in Washington Khidir Haroun Ahmed and his wife, Howaida, and Counselor at the London Embassy, Dr. El Sadiq Bakhiet. Assistant Keeper Jane Hogan at the University of Durham's Sudan Archive guided us through rich historical material. David Maurice of Seymour Travel in London got us the best fares possible to Sudan. We extend a special note of gratitude to Hussein Kheirelsid Babiker of the DAL Group, who handled an SUV over the desert with the same steady, reliable hand that he used to navigate Khartoum traffic.

Several scholars and friends, American as well as Sudanese, did us the favor of reading the manuscript. They include Dr. Amna Badri, Dr. David Decker, Dr. Francis Deng, Ms. Nancy Jackson, Dr. Richard Lobban, Dr. Carolyn Fluehr Lobban, Dr. Khalid al-Mubarak, and Dr. Mahgoub El-Tigani. Dr. Jafar Mirghani Ahmed of the Sudan Civilization Institute provided wise counsel throughout the two years it took to complete the book. These scholars kept us from making some serious errors of fact, and we are indebted to them. Suzanne Kotz did a fine job of editing the final drafts. We take complete responsibility for any mistakes left in the text or the photo captions.

Our deepest appreciation goes to Neyla Freeman, whose steadfast belief in this book, sound financial management, and superb eye for beauty in unexpected places kept us on track.

Finally, we thank Ed Marquand and his talented team at Marquand Books. They have guided us through the process and produced a book that we hope will make all Sudanese proud.

Timothy Carney, Victoria Butler, and Michael Freeman

With thanks and in recognition:

The DAL Group
The El Nefeidi Group
Golden Arrow Company, Ltd
Greater Nile Petroleum Company, Ltd

Mr. and Mrs. Fred L. Hanson
Hilton Khartoum
Mr. Noah A. Samara

El Nasr Construction Company

Higleig Petroleum Services

Creative Associates
Marilyn and Michael Dore
Dr. Hania Morsi Fadl
Mobitel
The SAMASU Group

Mr. Francis Schaffer
Mr. Minas Sitinas
SDV Transintra
Talisman Energy

Abdel Karim Mirghani Cultural Center
Amipharma Laboratories
Amzar Trading and Services
Ariab Mining Company Ltd
John and Kohar Bodourian
Development Alternatives International
Development Technology and Services
    International
Miles Donnelly and Tigani El Karib
Education Company for Investment and Trading
Ericsson
Giad for Automotive Industry Company
Rushdi and Julia Hamid
Mr. Mohamed Hieba
High-Tech Petroleum Company
Intercontinental Travels
International Resources Group
Karplen Consultants
Kenana Sugar Company Ltd

Charles and Norma Kfouri
KALZAC
Lundin Petroleum AB
Dr. Nabil Pharmaceuticals
Nile Spring Water
Mohamed Noor Opticians
Petrodar Operating Company
Petronas
Rumbek Rendezvous
Schaffer Global Group
Sheikan Insurance & Reinsurance Company, Ltd
The Shell Company of the Sudan, Ltd
SMT Engineering Company
Pieter and Rose Stapel
Sudana Electromechanical Company, Ltd
Sudapet
TNT
Vam Oil International, FZE
White Nile Petroleum Operating Company

BIBLIOGRAPHY

Adams, William Y. *Nubia: Corridor to Africa*. Princeton, N.J.: Princeton University Press, 1976.
Still a landmark and readable book for a wide-ranging understanding of Nubia, Sudan, and Egypt. Arabic translation by Mahgoub al-Tigani Mahmoud (Cairo, 2004).

Burr, J. Millard, and Robert O. Collins. *Requiem for the Sudan: War, Drought, and Disaster Relief on the Nile*. Boulder, Colo.: Westview Press, 1995.
Twenty years of modern Sudanese history, from 1972 to 1993, with a focus on the resumption of the civil war in 1983 and bilateral relations between Sudan and the U.S.

———. *Revolutionary Sudan: Hasan al-Turabi and the Islamist State, 1989–2000*. Leiden: Brill, 2003.
Burr and Collins inform about Sudan during the first decade of Islamist rule.

Deng, Francis. *War of Visions: Conflict of Identities in the Sudan*. Washington, D.C.: Brookings Institution, 1995.
Deng analyzes the north-south conflict as a function of the north's failure to accept Sudan's plurality and diversity.

Edwards, David N. *The Nubian Past: An Archaeology of the Sudan*. London and New York: Routledge, 2004.
A cutting-edge study in historical archaeology with thoughtful commentary on ethnicity.

Holt, P.M., and M.W. Daly. *A History of the Sudan: From the Coming of Islam to the Present Day*. 5th ed. Harlow, Eng. and New York: Longmans, 2000.
The indispensable guide to modern Sudanese history, with good maps.

Lobban, Richard, Robert Kramer, and Carolyn Fluehr-Lobban. *Historical Dictionary of the Sudan*. Lanham, Md.: Scarecrow Press, 2002.
Emphasis on post-independence Sudan, bringing clarity to what is a complicated picture. Useful bibliography and Internet sites.

Scroggins, Deborah. *Emma's War*. New York: Pantheon, 2002.
The civil war and the complexities of Sudan, through the real story of an aid worker's romantic delusions.

Welsby, Derek A., and Julie R. Anderson. *Sudan: Ancient Treasures*. London: British Museum, 2004.
A wonderfully illustrated and informative work with more than three hundred objects illustrating two hundred thousand years and text by fifty scholars of art, archaeology, and anthropology.

INDEX

Page numbers in **bold** indicate photographs or photographs and their caption text.

First published in the United Kingdom in 2005 by Thames & Hudson
Ltd, 181A High Holborn, London WC1V 7QX

www.thamesandhudson.com

British Library Cataloguing-in-Publication Data
A catalogue record for this book is available from the British Library

ISBN-13: 978-0-500-51257-9
ISBN-10: 0-500-51257-4

Page 1: Young Darfur woman, Tawila
Pages 2–3: The Egyptian Pharaoh Amenhotep III's "temple of a million
years" at Soleb on the northern Nile
Pages 4–5: Women from the Fur and Zagawa tribes at a refugee camp in
Darfur, September 2004
Pages 6–7: Burial pyramids at the royal necropolis of the kingdom of
Kush, Meroe, near Bejrawia
Page 8: Nuba girl at Keilak, south of the Nuba Mountains
Pages 10–11: Students in Malakal learn math in Arabic

Edited by Suzanne Kotz
Proofread by Barbara McGill
Indexed by Naomi Linzer
Designed by Jeff Wincapaw
Image postproduction by Yukako Shibata
Separations by iocolor, Seattle
Produced by Marquand Books, Inc., Seattle
    www.marquand.com
Printed in China by C&C Offset Printing Co., Ltd.